The "Strong Poet"

Studies in Inclusive Education

Series Editor

Roger Slee (*University of South Australia, Australia*)

Editorial Board

Mel Ainscow (*University of Manchester, UK*)
Felicity Armstrong (*Institute of Education, University of London, UK*)
Len Barton (*Institute of Education, University of London, UK*)
Suzanne Carrington (*Queensland University of Technology, Australia*)
Joanne Deppeler (*Monash University, Australia*)
Linda Graham (*Queensland University of Technology, Australia*)
Levan Lim (*National Institute of Education, Singapore*)
Missy Morton (*University of Canterbury, New Zealand*)

VOLUME 44

Critical Leaders and the Foundation of Disability Studies in Education

Series Editor

Linda Ware (*Independent Scholar*)

VOLUME 2

The titles published in this series are listed at *brill.com/clfd*

The "Strong Poet"

Essays in Honor of Lous Heshusius

Edited by

Linda Ware and Emily A. Nusbaum

BRILL
SENSE

LEIDEN | BOSTON

Cover illustration: *Lous Heshusius*, drawing by Elizabeth Edinger

All chapters in this book have undergone peer review.

The Library of Congress Cataloging-in-Publication Data is available online at http://catalog.loc.gov

Typeface for the Latin, Greek, and Cyrillic scripts: "Brill". See and download: brill.com/brill-typeface.

ISSN 2666-1772
ISBN 978-90-04-42726-6 (paperback)
ISBN 978-90-04-42727-3 (hardback)
ISBN 978-90-04-42728-0 (e-book)

Copyright 2020 by Koninklijke Brill NV, Leiden, The Netherlands, except where stated otherwise.
Koninklijke Brill NV incorporates the imprints Brill, Brill Hes & De Graaf, Brill Nijhoff, Brill Rodopi, Brill Sense, Hotei Publishing, mentis Verlag, Verlag Ferdinand Schöningh and Wilhelm Fink Verlag.
All rights reserved. No part of this publication may be reproduced, translated, stored in a retrieval system, or transmitted in any form or by any means, electronic, mechanical, photocopying, recording or otherwise, without prior written permission from the publisher.
Authorization to photocopy items for internal or personal use is granted by Koninklijke Brill NV provided that the appropriate fees are paid directly to The Copyright Clearance Center, 222 Rosewood Drive, Suite 910, Danvers, MA 01923, USA. Fees are subject to change.

This book is printed on acid-free paper and produced in a sustainable manner.

Contents

Series Introduction VII
  Linda Ware
Notes on Contributors XI

Introduction: Lous Heshusius, the "Strong Poet" 1
  Linda Ware and Emily A. Nusbaum

1 Boredom, Refusal, and Disbelief, Coming to the Work of Lous
  Heshusius 10
    Linda Ware

2 New to the "Family of Malcontents": Reflections on an Early Career of
  Creative Discontent 26
    Emily A. Nusbaum

3 Seeking the Real in an Unreal World on Reading Lous Heshusius 40
    Alicia A. Broderick

4 Reflexivity with and without Self: Lous Heshusius' Purposeless Listening
  Exercise 56
    Julie Allan

5 The Illusion of Our Separativeness: Exploring Heshusius' Concept
  of Participary Conciousness in Disability Research and Inclusive
  Education 72
    Deborah J. Gallagher

6 Respect for the Ghost, Justice for the Living: A Sociological Haunting
  30 Years in the Making 89
    Danielle M. Cowley

Index 121

Series Introduction

> Change is often unpredictable and indirect. We don't know the future. We've changed the world many times, and remembering that, *that history*, is really a source of power to continue and it doesn't get talked about nearly enough.
>
> REBECCA SOLNIT (2017, emphasis added)

∵

Critical Leaders and the Foundation of Disability Studies in Education aims to formalize the significance of early histories of understanding disability drawn from the scholarship of those who turned away from conventional status quo and pathologized constructs commonly accepted worldwide to explain disability in schools and society. The series begins with recognition of North American scholars including: Ellen Brantlinger, Lous Heshusius, Steve Taylor, Doug Biklen, and Thomas M. Skrtic. We will expand the series to include scholars from several international countries who likewise formed analyses that shaped the terrain for the emergence of critical perspectives that have endured and slowly given rise to the interdisciplinary field of Disability Studies in Education.

Critical Leaders and the Foundation of Disability Studies in Education singles out individuals who began their professional careers in the shadow of traditional special education research and practice. However at an important juncture, each forged a critical turn from status quo beliefs and practices about disability in schools and society. They dared to challenge the inherited orthodoxy of special education and through their individual and collective efforts professional criticism of special education grew in increasing larger circles among like minds. Their scholarship represents a persistent commitment to reconstruct the narrative in schools and society that marginalized children and minimized life opportunities for disabled people. Mapping their efforts over time, these individuals were subsequently distinguished as among the earliest voices of critical special education (Gallagher et al., 2004; Ware, 2001, 2004, 2017).

Each book began as an invited symposia presented at the annual meeting of the American Educational Research Association—beginning in 2012 and continuing to the present. The symposia panelists were invited to consider the influence made by each scholar featured in *Critical Leaders and the Foundation of Disability Studies in Education*.

The series unpacks the insights of these individuals—who initially worked in isolation—unaware of their common interests that would ultimately lead to this collective. Their thinking served as the initial grounding for disability studies in education despite the fact that none such community actually existed until late in the 1990s. Steven J. Taylor offered that many in this circle of critical special educators advanced disability studies in education "before it had a name" (Taylor, 2006, *Vital Questions Facing Disability Studies in Education*). He explained:

> [T]he key themes underlying Disability Studies in Education can be traced back many years before it was identified as an area of inquiry or associated with professional groups, conferences, and scholarly publications. Of course, in earlier times, some of these themes were not fully developed, and their implications not completely explored. Yet, an understanding of the intellectual forbearers of Disability Studies in Education can help us understand more clearly the foundational ideas underlying this area of scholarship. (p. xiii)

Critical Leaders and the Foundation of Disability Studies in Education articulates this history through the remembering, as Solnit suggested, of our history and to intentionally proclaim this history as a "source of power [that] doesn't get talked about nearly enough" (2017). The series weaves across decades to plot the arc of scholarly accomplishment, inviting readers to look back, while also looking forward in an attempt to build a more capacious and generative DSE community marked by its clear divergence from special education. The claim that "DSE is not SPED!" is a familiar rallying cry among our contemporaries, however, few are aware that Thomas M. Skrtic, writing in 1988, suggested that the "alternative paradigm" he outlined would give way to a discernable reorientation that would "produce a community of special education professionals who would think and act in ways substantially different from their contemporary counterparts" (p. 444).

Today, through professional affiliations and publications, Disability Studies in Education authorizes Skrtic's imagined future—a space for professionals who think and act in ways that differ substantially from those who align with special education. We articulate our commitment to:

> [U]nderstand disability from a social model perspective drawing on social, cultural, historical, discursive, philosophical, literary, aesthetic, artistic, and other traditions to challenge medical, scientific, and psychological models of disability as they relate to education. (Disability Stud-

ies in Education Special Interest Group, American Educational Research Association)

Disability Studies in Education makes specific the authority of an agenda to support the development of research, policy, and activism that:
- Contextualises disability within political and social spheres
- Privileges the interest, agendas, and voices of people labeled with disability/disabled people
- Promotes social justice, equitable and inclusive educational opportunities, and full and meaningful access to all aspects of society for people labeled with disability/disabled people
- Assumes competence and reject deficit models of disability.

Informed in a myriad of ways meticulously braided back to those who early on voiced dissent, discontent, and disavowal, Disability Studies in Education scholars have authored a resounding critique of education that pushes our thinking beyond the binary of the social/medical model debate located within the contexts of schooling—and special education in particular. Over two decades following on the "official" launch of the Disability Studies in Education Special Interest Group (SIG) in affiliation with the American Education Research Association, and the subsequent convening of the annual/bi-annual Disability Studies in Education conference co-hosted in partnership with various universities nationally and internationally, we advance a persistent critique of: classification schemes; categorization rituals; hostile behavior/reductionist practice; isolated/segregated/separate placements, and the unreflective and pervasive stigmatization of disabled children and youth embedded in the special education knowledge base. Each volume in this series reminds readers of the enduring influence and leadership of these critical special education scholars. Disability Studies in Education scholars whose work is cast within the shadows of this scholarly legacy are indebted to the bold and unrestrained thinking that remains provocative to this day.

Finally, the series aims to encourage future generations of scholars and educators to find their way "back" to Disability Studies in Education foundational knowledge sooner, rather than later in their careers. We recognize that the most courageous work remains ahead for budding scholars as they declare an explicit "anti-special education" focus in their research, scholarship and teaching. Understanding that individuals considered in this series made a critical turn away from the ideology that shaped special education orthodoxy (Gallagher et al., 2004), and as a consequence many mid-career and senior disability studies in education scholars forged a professional identity challenging status quo thinking about disability common in higher education and teacher preparation programs. Readers will find, we hope, power in knowing that perhaps we need not rage against the machine, yet, roar we must.

Critical Leaders and the Foundation of Disability Studies in Education provides purposeful connections to the wisdom and enduring ideas of these critical thinkers to reveal the depth of their imprint on current research in the field of disability studies in education. However, we caution that this series is not to be read as a compendium of their contributions. What we hope to encourage is that future generations of scholars will mine the original works of these scholars and excavate primary source materials in an effort to reinforce and renew the foundation of disability studies in education. It is a movement that will prosper when informed of its complex and confounding roots.

Linda Ware
Editor of *Critical Leaders and the Foundation of*
Disability Studies in Education

Notes on Contributors

Julie Allan

is Professor of Equity and Inclusion and Head of the School of Education at the University of Birmingham, UK. Her research focuses on inclusive education, disability studies and children's rights and she been advisor to the Scottish Parliament, the Welsh Assembly and the Dutch and Queensland Governments and Council of Europe. Her recent books include *Psychopathology at School: Theorising Mental Disorder in Education* (with Valerie Harwood; Routledge, 2014) and the 2020 *Routledge World Yearbook in Education – Schooling, Governance and Inequalities* (with Valerie Harwood and Clara Rübner Jorgensen; Routledge, 2020).

Alicia A. Broderick

is a Professor of Education in the College of Education and Human Services at Montclair State University, New Jersey, USA. Her work deploys Disability Studies (DS), in intersection with other critical conceptual frameworks, in critiquing the structural inequities inherent in formal, compulsory education systems, as well as in exploring the potential for more liberatory learning and living outside of those systems. She is additionally engaged in an ongoing critical analysis of the intersections of behaviorism and capitalism underlying what she terms the Autism Industrial Complex.

Danielle M. Cowley

is an Associate Professor in the Department of Special Education at the University of Northern Iowa. Her primary teaching responsibilities include undergraduate teacher preparation courses in the areas of humanistic approaches to behavior, educational and post-school transitions, differentiated instruction, and best practices for inclusion. Dr. Cowley's research interests include inclusive education, disability studies in education, urban school reform, gender in schooling, and culturally responsive transition programming. She has published several book chapters and in journals such as *PowerPlay: A Journal of Educational Justice,* the *Journal of Literary and Cultural Disability Studies* and the *International Journal of Development, Disability, and Education*, and has presented her research at numerous national and regional conferences. Dr. Cowley was the recipient of the 2014 AERA-sponsored Disability Studies in Education Outstanding Dissertation Award for her research with adolescent girls with disabilities.

Deborah J. Gallagher

is Professor of Education at the University of Northern Iowa. Her research interest centers on the philosophy of science as it pertains to research on disability, pedagogy, and policy in education and special education.

Emily A. Nusbaum

is an Assistant Professor at University of San Francisco. She has won awards for her dissertation and early career contributions to disability studies in education and social justice initiatives. Emily teaches graduate courses in DSE and critical, qualitative research.

Linda Ware

Independent Scholar, survived a lengthy academic career at universities from New Mexico to New York. Her publications appeared in prestigious national and international academic journals. In addition to this series, *Critical Leaders and the Foundation of Disability Studies in Education*, she edited *Ideology and the Politics of (In)Exclusion* (Peter Lang, 2004) and most recently *Critical Readings in Interdisciplinary Disability Studies: (Dis)assemblages* (Springer, 2020). She is also a Section Editor for *Beginning with Disability: A Primer* (Routledge, 2017, L. J. Davis, Editor). Linda happily resides near Santa Fe, New Mexico.

INTRODUCTION

Lous Heshusius, the "Strong Poet"

Linda Ware and Emily A. Nusbaum

The "Strong Poet": Essays in Honor of Lous Heshusius celebrates the research and scholarship of one of the earliest advocates for fundamental change in the field of special education in the mid-to-late twentieth century. She began her career as an Assistant Professor in the Department of Teaching and the Department of Special Education, at the University Northern of Iowa. During that period, she authored numerous works critical of traditional special education despite the fact that she was on the faculty of a very traditional special education program. Some years later she left the United States and relocated to Canada to teach at York University where she remained until she retired as Emeritus Professor. Heshusius brought to her academic career, experience as a teacher versed in the principles of inclusion at a time when this concept had yet to be explored and the term had yet to be coined. And to this day, the full value of "inclusion" has yet to be realized. Heshusius' doctoral research was unique then, and now, in that she crafted a qualitative research inquiry into the lives of young adults navigating adulthood in a group home residence during the late 1960s and early 1970s. Published as *Meaning in Life as Experienced by Persons Labeled Retarded in a Group Home* (Heshusius, 1981), her research served as the gateway to merge several strands of intellectual pursuits. Most critically, she pointed to the impact of social stigma on marginalized populations who were removed from social spaces and in so doing denied the opportunity to thrive in social worlds they could not claim, must less shape. It was equally important that Heshusius embraced qualitative research methods as the path to probe particulate understandings and misunderstandings at the nexus of socially constructed attitudes, beliefs and assumptions in the example of disability. She published her research with Charles C. Thomas, LTD, a respected publishing house known for its "specialty titles and textbooks in the biomedical sciences, behavioral sciences, education and special education, speech-language and hearing, as well as rehabilitation and long-term care" (Publishersarchive.com/publisher, 2018). Following the publication of her research Heshusius joined an emergent community of qualitative researchers who challenged status quo educational research exclusively rooted in large-scale quantitative research studies. It bears mention that Heshusius remained among a handful of qualitative researchers who applied inquiry into the lives

© KONINKLIJKE BRILL NV, LEIDEN, 2020 | DOI: 10.1163/9789004427280_001

of disabled individuals. She challenged the firmly drawn lines that "boxed in" disabled individuals beneath the lowest bar. She aimed to articulate and challenge the limits of the ubiquitous deficiency frame from which educational and rehabilitative researchers relied upon to explore the lives of those society named disabled and disposable.

Her inquiry began with the presumption of competence informed by the scholarship of the anthropologist, R. B. Edgerton, and in particular, *The Cloak of Competence: Stigma in the Lives of the Mentally Retarded* (1967). Edgerton's groundbreaking research inspired Heshusius in her study of the ways that individuals living in a group home setting made "meaning" or the "lack of meaning" of their lives in institutional care (1981, p. vi). Her qualitative methodological approach began with actually listening to the accounts offered by her research participants and with the assumption that her research participants possessed the wherewithal and agency to articulate a perspective on their lives. Such an orientation was far from the norm in the example of research "on" rather than "with" disabled individuals. Throughout her career, Heshusius called for researchers, educators and others across the professional support services community who worked with disabled children and adults to reflect on a very simple question: "Why do we more often than not stand in the way of these persons' search for more meaningful living?" (p. vii). Indeed, it was this early research with young adults that set the compass for Heshusius' life-long quest to privilege the voice of individuals with disabilities through qualitative inquiry. Was it merely coincidence that this nascent conversation on qualitative and interpretive research in educational research was brewing? After all Heshusius conducted her doctoral research in the late 1960s and early 1970s ahead of the conversation on "alternative" research methods in the decades that followed (Gage, 1989; Lincoln, 1985; Guba & Lincoln, 1985; Skrtic, 1986). She advanced a shift from the mindset of training and behavioral conditioning upon unwitting disabled children and youth to one that assumed the capacity to learn, love, desire and even demand the right to live in the world. Such a simple assumption, but some would argue today, this remains as revolutionary today as it was 50 years ago. As this perspective served to guide her advocacy, she is recognized now as among the preeminent voices of what came to be known as a DSE perspective. This series and the contributors to this volume in particular attest to the myriad ways that Heshusisus opened doors for researchers and scholars to challenge conventional attitudes, assumptions and beliefs about disability and disabled children, youth and adults.

Throughout her career, Heshusius voiced a strong, yet poetic critique about the limits of general and special education in an era when the later was advanced as "the way" to ensure the hard-won right to an equitable education for disabled children. For Heshusius hers was a critique that insisted upon

LOUS HESHUSIUS, THE "STRONG POET"

deeper understanding about rationality and the need to make somatic sense. Writing along with her co-editor, Keith Ballard in the introduction to their book, *From Positivism to Intrepretivism and Beyond, Tales of Transformation in Educational and Social Research* (1996), they conveyed the (dis)ease they experienced with status quo special education policy, practice and the beliefs it promulgated about disability.

> When we started to consciously reflect on how we had changed our most basic beliefs, we had to acknowledge that we knew, before we could account for it intellectually, that we no longer believed in what we were doing or in what we being taught. That is, while the dominant assumptions still made sense rationally in terms of how things are done, they no longer made sense somatically and affectively. Something felt wrong. Our bodies told us so. (p. 2)

Heshusius and Ballard captured what many contributors to this book recognized when trying to find the words to resist status quo thinking about disability, while simultaneously celebrating the discovery of like-minded colleagues. Today, scholars who identify beneath the banner of disability studies rather than special education recognize this project was about so much more than a paradigm change. In particular, Broderick (in this volume), speaks of the spiritual renewal following her introduction to Heshusius, and to the book co-edited with Ballard (1996).

Heshusius continues to critique the dominant positivist paradigm for understanding diverse human experience and not only in the instance of special education. Of late, she has turned her attention to the excavation of first person experience among those living with chronic pain whose narratives are chronicled in her most recent publications (Heshusius, 2009, 2017). Following a near fatal automobile accident in 1996 and the on-going recovery that followed, Heshusius turned to auto-ethnographic inquiry and the exploration of the worlds of pain and chronic pain management. Readers will discover how Heshusius navigates the world of chronic pain management, a world that she found strikingly similar in its foundational principles to those very same principles she critiqued in special education: A world similarly in need of humanization.

1   **Chapter Overviews**

Chapter 1 describes how, as a classroom teacher, Linda Ware found her way to the writing of Lous Heshusius. It was early in Ware's teaching career as a middle school resource teacher that Ware happened onto the debate over holism and the challenge it posed to learning context for students identified with disabilities and to the preparation of teachers. Tracing back in time to a period marked by the "roll-out" of Distar and the promise of boxed curriculum, it was quite by accident that Ware discovered the first wave of critical special education scholars. The chapter stands apart from the others in this collection as it was composed retrospectively from reflections on the ways that Heshusius impacted Ware as a novice public schoolteacher in El Paso, Texas. Ware revisited her own trajectory from a K-12 teacher to a disability studies scholar, to signal the ways that Heshusius, the "strong poet" was lodged deep into the soul of teachers. Ware maps the beginnings of what became a strong influence on her public school teaching, her doctoral research, and through various funded projects, her passion to introduce Heshusius to audiences that might not have discovered the relevance of her scholarship (Ware, 2000; Mitchell, Snyder, & Ware, 2008, 2014). Revisiting this early writing of Heshusius against her own early career context Ware found the seeds of her bold declaration to reject a professional special education identity and to instead push against the claim that disability studies in education as a field would succeed only if it bridged with special education. Ware successfully collaborated with colleagues outside schools of education to develop undergraduate programs in disability studies to establish a program of study open to all students and not exclusively to those in education. In this way, she hoped to engage students across rigid boundaries and disciplines that ultimately proved to challenge the academy's predilection to ghettoize programs (see Ware, 2017, in Davis). Although Ware won competitive grants from the Spencer Foundation (1999[1]) and the National Endowment for the Humanities (2000,[2] 2001,[3] 2002[4]) and in 2003 with colleagues David T. Mitchell and Sharon L. Snyder[5] to advance more critical and contemporary understanding of disability, her work was often at odds within the academic settings in which she worked—specifically, schools of education intolerant of educational inclusion and disability studies. Over the years, it was mentorship by Heshusius that led Ware to "connect the dots" in debate over ideological shifts in the understanding of disability as more than a problem posed to teachers, families and to individuals. Ware maintains a life-long friendship with Heshusius—always comforted by her guidance.

Chapter 2 considers Emily Nusbaum's translation and application of "deep listening" and a more close reading of the social context advanced by Heshusius. Nusbaum returns to her own early career experience wherein she embraced the interpretive impulse as a consultant and advocate for disabled children and their families seeking access to mainstream classrooms and school-based supports. She describes one particular Individualized Education Plan (IEP) meeting in which her goal was to document the humanity of Lelia, an eighth-grade student through carefully chosen examples to substantiate that, which was so obvious to Nusbaum, yet routinely overlooked by the school psychologists. Lelia was clearly more than the sum of the psychologist's boxes that were checked to categorize her with "severe retardation," "blindness," and "significant hearing loss." In contrast, Nusbaum provided a report informed by a close reading of Lelia through the lens of her "unique embodiment." In the process of reading that report it became uncomfortable for everyone, including Nusbaum to move away from the singular focus on medicalized diagnosis and prognosis. Despite Nusbaum's nuanced account of human dignity and worth much of Lelia remained unseen by the professionals:

> ... the way her body moved in response to the different vocalizations Lelia made when friends met her at the bus versus when an aide told her it was time to go to the bathroom as she was wheeled out of her classroom ... her visible excitement when she heard the voice of her teacher come into the classroom each morning.

That Lelia might contribute to the community of her classroom, school and family was unrecognizable and of little consequence among the professionals charged to decide a child's fate. Lelia was reduced to the assessor's notation of scores and rankings reported as "age equivalents in development to a child under one year old ... no more than a vegetable." In one simple and cogent claim, Nusbaum tells us that her final pitch—a heartfelt, yet intellectual appeal—was no more complicated than the observation that, "Lelia's humanness was evident in other's care for and consideration of her, of what she contributed, and that her presence was missed when she was not there." Writing well after her initial exposure in graduate school to the scholarship of Heshusius, Nusbaum concurred that, at the "heart" of the advocacy dilemma for those unable to dismantle a system-wide mechanistic worldview in the example of disability, "the danger lies in letting such things have a life of their own" (Heshusius, 1982, p. 10).

Chapter 3 affords a similar glimpse into the frustration faced by Alicia Broderick, when early in her career as a consultant she supported a young student with behavioral issues associated with autism. Broderick was versed in Applied Behavioral Analysis (ABA) and certified to devise individual interventions and came to an ideological impasse in the presence of the child and his family. Similar to Ware and Nusbaum who peered into those spaces where Heshusius' notation of "epistemological incongruence" was layered in the vastness of unreflective schooling practices, Broderick recognized much of the same redundancy in an educational system she describes as rife with "ontological violence." This early career assignment troubled Broderick for years as she continued to experience that same "knowing" that something was not right, but before she could account for it intellectually (Heshusius & Ballard, 1996). This phenomenon, the paradigmatic transition from positivism to interpretivism, was framed as a "fundamental deconstruction and reconstruction of agreements about what counts as real and how we allow each other to claim knowledge" (p. 4). For Broderick, coming to this insight followed years of frustration with educational systems and special education in particular. It is was with great irony that she found reading Heshusius and wondering, "whence came Heshusius' optimism, her joy, her 'loving [of] the journey however difficult it has been?" (1996, p. 54).

Chapter 4 affords to Julie Allan, the opportunity to lead readers through an activity undertaken with thirteen undergraduate teacher education students, informed by Heshusius' notion of "participatory consciousness" (1995). The future teachers were encouraged to probe their own biases about students and their lives through unstructured conversations with young, disabled people. Allan leans into an important conversation in disability studies in education regarding student teachers' understanding of medical and social models of disability as an intellectual space necessary to explore from the inside out. Allan found that although her students were quick to memorize the definitions of key concepts in disability studies, contextualizing them in educational practice proved to be more daunting. More often than not, special educators must comply with the mandate to medicalize disability and cast it within the realm of remediation and cure/deficit discourses as they move through their coursework. Many student teachers lack the confidence to trouble differing modes of understanding disability. Typical practice affords special educators the opportunity to rehearse the "hunt for disability" (Baker, 2002; Graham, 2014) and to prize the pathologizing of disability throughout their teacher preparation coursework (Broderick & Lalavani, 2017), reflecting the inherited and often, uninterrogated P-12 conversations on disability reify the problem of difference (Lalavani, 2015; Ware, 2017). Allan offers teachers a way into exploring unconscious biases about students and their lives that may initially be difficult to name—although necessary to explore, through a listening exercise that does not exclude listening to self in a kind of "reflexivity that had at its heart a concern with power relations" (p. 10).

Chapter 5 follows a related line of discussion situated within teacher preparation as Deborah J. Gallagher turns her attention to the persistent debate over the "centrality of methods and techniques" and the "what works" debate linked to Heshusius' often cited *Educational Researcher* article, "Freeing Ourselves from Objectivity: Managing Subjectivity or Turning Toward a Participatory

LOUS HESHUSIUS, THE "STRONG POET"

Mode of Consciousness" (1994). In much the same way each chapter makes clear, reflexive analysis must become the default stance for honest exploration of that which troubles us and alienates us from deeper understanding about disability, our students and the teaching process. Gallagher recognized that her own philosophical treatment of the objectivity/subjectivity debates relative to how we come to know what we believe paled in comparison to the thorough treatment Heshusius offered in this article alone. And yet, as Gallagher reminds, Lous failed to achieve "immediate acceptance" among researchers and teachers. This point underscores the significance of launching this series beginning with Lous Heshusius because there is consensus that:

> her ideas have been "too original—too unapologetically nonconforming in ways that deftly permeate well beyond the surface of the subject matter at hand. Not unexpectedly, those who are quite satisfied with (and invested in) the institutionally established ways of doing and thinking find Hesusius's work decidedly unappealing. It has just the opposite effect on those who are searching, or who have searched, for more morally satisfying answers.

Chapter 6 provides yet another, equally intimate exchange by Danielle Cowley who crafted a letter to Lous, as if "in conversation" with a close friend and confidant. Cowley was not a panelist on the original AERA symposium, but was included following her recognition for the 2015 outstanding dissertation award from the Disability Studies in Education Special Interest Group at AERA. One of us (Ware) recognized obvious parallels between Cowley's doctoral research and that conducted by Lous in the late 1970s as both expressed deep emotional connection to the participants that informed their research. For Cowley, the letter writing experience extended her thinking at a critical juncture as she embarked on her career, uncertain of how she would advance the risky endeavor of passionate scholarship. In much the same way that Ware described her earliest desire to win "imagined" approbation from Lous, Cowley's letter speaks to the importance of finding and sustaining collegial support at an early career juncture. Many of us work as the lone DSE scholar within a traditional special education department secure in its rejection of inclusive ideology and absolute dismissal of the belief that disability need not be shaped by the rhetoric of "difference as problem" (Ware, 2005; 2017; Ware & Valle, 2010). The professional camaraderie that DSE has fostered for this generation of scholars was not afforded to Heshusius, and yet to this day, she provides unique mentorship through her scholarship to many who proudly identify as DSE scholars.

2 Conclusion

The contributors to this book were not students of Lous Heshusius in the conventional way as none received university instruction from her. Some came to her work in the throes of frustration and discontent as doctoral students, as newly minted tenure track faculty, as educational researchers, or as a colleague in the example of Deborah J. Gallagher who worked with Lous at the University of Iowa. Each came to the desire to distance themselves from the positivist and behaviorist status quo thinking that was, and remains to this day, endemic to the field of special education. The contributors also offer a glimpse into the tension of teaching in academic programs that preserve special education's normative practices and signal the ways resistance operates within their own teaching, research and scholarship. As editors, we believe that this series will reinforce our authority to imagine disability otherwise and to challenge the misalignment of institutionalized special education ideology with those enduring perspectives that are the bedrock of DSE.

Notes

1 Ideology and the Politics of Inclusion ($50,000.00). Spencer Foundation, Research Conference Award, Project PI, 1999–2000.
2 Summer Institute on Disability Studies, Fellowship Award ($3,500.00). National Endowment for the Humanities. San Francisco State University, San Francisco, California, 2000.
3 University of Rochester Committee on Interdisciplinary Studies: Disability Studies Cluster ($3,600.00 annual award). University of Rochester, 2001.
4 A Collaborative Inquiry on Understanding Disability in Secondary and Post-Secondary Settings ($25,000.00). Project PI. National Endowment for the Humanities, Research Focus Grant, 2000–2001.
5 Integrating Disability Studies into Secondary Education Curricula. National Endowment for the Humanities Summer Institute for Teachers ($189,000.00). Co-director with David T. Mitchell and Sharon L. Snyder, University of Illinois, Chicago, 2003.

References

Broderick, A., & Lalvani, P. (2017). Dysconscious ableism: Toward a liberatory praxis in teacher education. *International Journal of Inclusive Education* (Online publication). http://dx.doi.org/10.1080/13603116.2017.1296034

Edgerton, R. B. (1967). *Cloak of competence*. Berkeley, CA: University of California Press.

Gage, N. L. (1989). The paradigm wars and their aftermath: A "historical" sketch of research in teaching since 1989. *Educational Researcher, 18*(7), 4–10.

Heshusius, L. (1981). *Meaning in life as experienced by persons labeled retarded in a group home.* Springfield, IL: Charles C. Thomas.

Lincoln, Y. S. (1985). *Organizational theory and inquiry: The paradigm revolution.* Beverly Hills, CA: Sage Publications.

Lincoln, Y. S., & Guba, E. G. (1985). *Naturalistic inquiry.* Beverly Hills, CA: Sage Publications.

Mitchell, D. T., Snyder, S. L., & Ware, L. (2014). Curricular cripistemologies: Or every child left behind. *Journal of Literary and Cultural Disability Studies, 8*(3), 301–319.

Skrtic, T. M. (1986). The crisis in special education knowledge: A perspective on perspective. *Focus on Exceptional Children, 18*(7), 1–16.

Ware, L. (2005). Many possible futures, many different directions: Merging critical special education and disability studies. In S. L. Gabel (Ed.), *Disability studies in education: Readings in theory and method* (pp. 103–124). New York, NY: Peter Lang.

Ware, L., & Valle, J. (2010). How do we begin a conversation on disability in urban education? In S. Steinberg (Ed.), *19 Urban questions teaching in the city* (pp. 113–130). New York, NY: Peter Lang.

CHAPTER 1

Boredom, Refusal, and Disbelief, Coming to the Work of Lous Heshusius

Linda Ware

Abstract

This chapter revisits the imprint made by the early writings of Lous Heshusius on the public school teaching and ideological positioning of the author, Linda Ware—then, a middle school resource room teacher and a parent to her young son enrolled in special education. Heshusius' insights stood in marked contrast to the professional literature and practices in teacher training programs. Heshusius amplified Ware's experience as a mother and as a teacher, inspiring what became Ware's critique of special education's misguided ideology.

Keywords

holism – teacher preparation – curriculum – first wave critical special education

1   Introduction

This chapter revisits the early influence of Lous Heshusius for this author when she was a middle school teacher, early in her career and unversed in the theory of Holism and the then-emergent critique of special education. Although dissatisfied with the paradigm that drove policy and practice in special education, this author was catapulted into a conversation on teaching, learning, and understanding disability in schools and society that remained an influence throughout her career. Early work by Heshusius led the author to question institutional injustice in the example of special education—questions that were too often overlooked, ignored, disavowed—and destructive to status quo beliefs about disability.

DISTAR. Direct Instruction System for Teaching Arithmetic and Reading (needed)—that's how I came to the work of Lous Heshusius. I was a middle school special education teacher in a suburban district in the Southwest, attending a mandatory "professional" training day focused on *DISTAR*.[1] District supervisors and teachers filled the "multi-use" auditorium, a former art house movie theatre in an upscale mall that had been repurposed to serve as the new district office. In the same space where I had previously enjoyed the films of Pedro Almovodar, Ken Loach, Mike Leigh and others, a mind-numbing direct-instruction-program presentation by district personnel took centre stage. Hours into the full-day session, I slipped away to explore the nearby professional library where, in prominent display on the circulation desk, I noticed the latest issue of *Learning Disability Quarterly* (LDQ, 1984). Its bold blue-edged cover and oversized block text read *Special Issue:* HOLISM.

I held two education degrees by that time and "Holism" held absolutely no meaning. I scanned the *LDQ* table of contents, hoping for clarity: "Special Education as a Moral Enterprise" (Altman); "Teacher Perceptions and Observed Outcomes: An Ethnographic Study of Classroom Interactions" (Miramontes, Chen, & Trueba), and "Why Would They and I Want to Do It? A Phenomenological-Theoretical View of Special Education" (Heshusius). Mary S. Poplin, the special issue editor, explained, "Holism is sweeping almost every field of inquiry—from physics to education, from philosophy to medicine" (1984, p. 290). Each contributor articulated a view on learning disabilities as "outside the usual perspectives of legalities, identification, and methodologies ... [and instead] as interactions between the school, the individual student, and society at large" (Poplin, 1984, p. 290). Each refuted the "reductionist manner in which we (educators) have conceptualized the content and context of the teaching/learning process" (Poplin, 1984, p. 291). Holism offered a counter-narrative to research and learning in a number of fields that ranged from "physics to education, from philosophy to medicine" (Poplin, 1984, p. 290).
Holism challenged hierarchies and structures that demanded incisive and often intrusive approaches to control and measure phenomena that by their nature are integrated and holistic. Holism diverged from the typical fare this professional journal and many others routinely published in allegiance to psychometric, pathological, and reductionist frames for research and instructional approaches. The special issue represented a dramatic shift from status quo thinking about disability that had long since located the "problem" of disability within the child and/or within the family. Such a perspective clashed with the ideology that produced DISTAR and other prescriptive instruction programs that were uniformly embraced by special education programs then (and to this day).

I was already a practitioner before I realized that holism had been elided, by design, from my university coursework. Behaviorism and the mechanistic approach to teaching and learning was the exclusive and unquestioned foundation for my entire teacher-preparation program. One of my special education professors earned her doctorate from the University of Oregon and often boasted of her mentorship from Carl Bereiter and Siegfried Engleman—the founding fathers of Direct Instruction (DI). In retrospect, as a newly certified teacher, I unwittingly accepted this positivist knowledge base that reified reductionist attitudes, assumptions, and practice in special education. Its legitimacy was uncontested science. Yet I was also the parent of a young son with disability and in that context, I intuitively refused behaviorism as wholly inadequate to my preferred parenting style and how I structured his learning experiences. Without fully understanding why, I intuitively knew that there was something misguided by a behaviorist paradigm. Later, when I realized the power of paradigms to contain and/or constrain our beliefs and actions, I claimed the right to disbelieve and the right to refuse the norms of practice.

The *LDQ Special Issue* proved to be the trapdoor from which I could emerge to engage in a new conversation on disability with contributors who were unwavering in their support of holism. *LDQ* introduced this multi-voiced debate on *alternative* paradigms for professional practice and policy in special education. I read the entire journal in one sitting that day and returned to the DISTAR workshop just in time for the closing comments. I was deeply impacted by the readings and lost in my own questions: *How had this critique emerged? What might it mean for my teaching? Why was I just now learning about this? Where would I find others willing to explore this with me as a practitioner and a parent?* One thing seemed certain—there was a movement afoot in special education that was critical of reductionism, positivism, and the unquestioned assumption that a scientific basis for teaching was beyond reproach. This special issue appeared at a critical juncture for me as I began my fifth year of teaching and my tenth year of parenting. I began a slow march away from institutional structures that framed special education as a project of rehabilitative cure and care, steeped in legal mandates far removed from supporting the whole child as a vibrant individual, worthy to be in the world.

2   The Introduction of Alternative Paradigms in Special Education

The *LDQ* contributors were part of a growing movement of an "emergent" critique of special education in the US and the UK (Barton & Tomlinson, 1984; Biklen & Bogdan, 1977; Blatt, 1972; Bogdan, 1982; Bogdan & Kuglemass, 1984; Bogdan & Taylor, 1976; Reynolds & Wang, 1983) that grew even more spirited following thereafter (Biklen, 1985; Bogdan & Knoll, 1988; Iano, 1986; Schwandt, 1988; Skrtic, 1986, 1987, 1988, 1990). These respected scholars won recognition as special education's early "alternative thinkers" who authored a critique of traditional attitudes, beliefs, practice, and policy. Their perspectives emerged from various academic homes—not exclusively special education, but each with attention to and interest in disability. This conversation signalled that which Thomas Skrtic referred to as the "multi-paradigmatic shift" in special education and disability research (1986, 1988, 1992). The multi-layered locations of this critique would fortify collective criticism, wherein no singular paradigm would carry the weight of an ideological shift, nor was any singular voice privileged. Skrtic (1988) predicted that this intellectual debate would "produce a community of special education professionals who would think and act in ways substantially different from their contemporary counterparts" (p. 444).

Holism would become one such example. In contrast to reductionism, holism reinforced the belief that context matters and that educational interventions could not be assumed to work with *all* learners in *all* settings as reductionism had long advanced. Heshusius had previously called attention to "paradigmatic conflict" in special education professional practice as the result of out-dated and exclusively "mechanistic assumptions about behaviour, teaching, and learning—and not learning—that underlie the conflict" (1982, p. 6). Poplin (1984c) counter-posed holism to reductionism to underscore its meaning in practice to identify critical faults:

1. The learning process is divided into segments, that is, discrete psychological processes such as auditory discrimination, discrete behaviors defined as instructional objectives, specific study skills, or cognitive strategies, and/or hierarchical developmental stages.
2. Instruction is primarily devoted to increasing a student's competence in school goals rather than life goals. Hence, there is little, if any, acknowledgment that school goals and life requirements may not coincide.
3. Assessment, evaluation, and special instruction are conducted almost solely for the purpose of seeking and remediating deficits; each activity is deficit driven.
4. The skills to be learned (i.e., information processing, academic behaviors, strategies, or study skills) are determined by the school (e.g., materials, procedures, educational administrators in local, state, and federal agencies, curriculum directors, and/or teachers). No consideration is given individual learners except that they may be assigned different parts of the prearranged set of essential or basic skills.
5. It is assumed that there are right and wrong ways to process information, to perform certain tasks, and to answer certain questions. However, the possibility is not considered that different people may validly comprehend various phenomena differently, or that facts change as our minds and knowledge evolve (cf. Newtonian physics and Einstein's physics of relativity) (p. 291).

Like Heshusius, Poplin identified special education paradigmatic assumptions in practice as problematic although neither faulted teachers in naming this core issue. Theirs was a critique of the system and its inability to recognize and respond to the *complexity* of teaching and learning—and by turns, to the *complexity* of humans in engagement with the world—as the more valuable end goal (emphasis added). Heshusius (1984) noted as problematic that:

> Teaching and learning are reduced to the level of rules and instrumentality, the most subordinate level in the hierarchy of ways by which we know. Because of the required quantification and measurement, teaching and learning often do not operate at the levels of what is meaningful to the child and what is worthwhile in the first place. (p. 7)

Poplin (1984) noted as problematic the fact that when teachers operate as technicians rather than informed professionals, they are compelled to:

> design curricula into which all students must fit [rather] than to learn about students' natural interests and proclivities before developing an intervention that permits them to apply their own experiences and languages to their learning. (p. 291)

And further, Poplin (1984) noted the damage that accrues to both teacher and learner in such circumstances, drawing a comparison that remains as relevant today as it was then:

> Standardizing the teaching process through basal readers or basic-skills curricula allows little teacher intuition or creativity just as using worksheets for instruction elicits little student spontaneity or creativity. (p. 291)

By my own example, I was expected to perform as a teacher in ways that I refused when teaching and parenting my own son, who was diagnosed with "cerebral palsy-like" symptoms. I determined early in his life that I would support his embrace of the world through experiences that inspired learning at the same time, mining his interests in meaningful ways. Through multiple and varied exposures to words, images, language, and especially music I found little need to drill him or reduce learning to its smallest bits in a task-analysis breakdown. Yet, in my day job, the reverse was engineered by the ubiquitous boxed curriculum, rooted to a paradigm that fell short in practice.

BOREDOM, REFUSAL, AND DISBELIEF

2.1   *Norms of Practice, the Boxed Curriculum*

At this moment, when some special educators were prompted to question the default to positivism, similar concerns by general educators surfaced. The well-respected, educational anthropologist and classroom-based researcher Courtney Cazden (1983) challenged the inadequacy of positivist social science approaches to curriculum design because it "can only be implemented in an authoritarian, manipulative, bureaucratic system" (p. 33). In fact, boxed curriculum and scripted teacher-proof materials for use by general and special educators were commonly adopted district-wide, and in the absence of teacher review. Such policy contributed to the "deskilling" of the teaching profession, so named by educational anthropologists and sociologists of education dating back to the 1970s (Giroux, Shor, etc.). The deskilling of teachers remains a critical conversation today—some 40 years later—as educators and schooling systems are more deeply embedded in bureaucratic control whether by states or at the local, district level of governance.[2] Setting aside the issue of bureaucratic forces, Heshusius (1984) disparaged norms of practice in which "programmed and sequenced materials, the worksheets, the remedial training models and approaches were so often used as ends in themselves" (p. 363). She insisted, "They have no real sense, they make no sense—they are non-sensible" (pp. 363–364). The non-sense and meaninglessness of positivist and reductionist approaches to student learning and teacher preparation was central to my own dis-ease with mandated district and state-wide reform initiatives. It was obvious that were students to be able to experience full educational opportunity, my own curriculum would need to tap into their lives and their interests— rarely evidenced in the published materials I was expected to utilize.

2.2   *The Irrelevance of Relevance*

As a middle school resource room teacher in the 1980s, I boldly resisted the use of the boxed curriculum and workbooks. This position was prompted by necessity, as my first teaching placement was in a school that was literally along the border between El Paso and Mexico. When I stopped by unannounced over the summer to see my classroom and sort through the classroom materials I imagined I would find, the assistant principal explained there were none. The process, he explained, would entail ordering materials through a resource/materials library once the final enrolment period ended. Given the combination of our proximity to the United States and Mexico border that necessitated proof of residency, the principal informed me that my final class size would likely be delayed by weeks. The district office, as a consequence, withheld a final budget because the state withheld its allocation pending the final headcount. In the meantime, the expectation, as noted by the assistant principal, was to "keep the students from killing one another!" As if on cue, he reached into an empty closet and retrieved a baseball bat left behind by the last teacher. Although he was, I believed, joking, this exchange proved to be a remarkable twist of fate: the barren shelves, the low bar for student learning, and the assumed irrelevance of my teaching propelled my desire to develop original teaching materials to get us through the weeks that it would take to verify district residency and obtain a final class size prior to ordering materials.

By necessity I appropriated the language of "individualized" instruction for my students and designed a curriculum that integrated contemporary music, films, current events, and technology that simultaneously addressed IEP goals and objectives. I drew on the richness of my students' ethnic and racial backgrounds as sources to influence reading and writing assignments that would motivate them to reclaim their abilities as learners. It was a curriculum to teach about the world that was similar to what I explored with my son and yet it was quite distinct from the standard-issue materials purported to address the individualized needs of disabled children and youth. Today such content would fall beneath the umbrella of inclusive pedagogy, culturally responsive teaching, differentiated instruction, justice pedagogy, etc.; however, at the time, it was uncommon for special educators to venture beyond the prescriptive boxed curriculum and dilapidated "kits" that lined the shelves of the district office resource materials library. This reality stood in contrast to Heshusius' words that the "teacher and student need to be able to perceive their activities as meaningful in the context of their academic and personal lives" (1982, p. 10).

2.3 Pedagogy and Principles

The curriculum I built over several years as a special education resource room teacher focused on problem-solving software, basic spreadsheet/database/ word processing applications, and Logo. Developed by Seymour Papert, a mathematician and protégé of Jean Piaget, Logo was a programming language that drew heavily on constructionism. Logo enabled young children to learn simple programming commands and sequences to create graphics and animation within a learning context that was deeply driven by logic and problem solving. This was far from the typical fare that students with disabilities experienced in schools. For my students, problem solving was intuitive and self-directed and created the conditions for autonomous learning. For my middle school students, primarily those identified with learning disabilities, Logo revealed the power of expressing their learning ability and a creative capacity to engage problem-solving skills that had not been tapped over prior years of schooling. That they were very much able to think and learn despite the labels placed upon them by the schools proved to be a source of confidence and renewed commitment to learning (Ware, 1989). For my son, the power to "think through movement" proved to be learning—given his mobility needs—that mattered on a deeper level. It was on the basis of this curriculum that I responded to a national call for special education teachers who utilized computers for other than drill and practice applications—the norm in most general and special education classrooms at the time. My program became part of a federally funded research project based in Cambridge, Massachusetts. It was only then that district interest in the content of my teaching emerged.[3] My immediate district-level supervisors often acknowledged that the classroom climate appeared "lively, creative, and welcoming" for students; however, they remained generally uncurious about my pedagogy and the ways students demonstrated learning. I was praised for timely and thorough completion of paperwork to document regulatory and procedural compliance, but students' active learning seemed less important. My performance evaluations were tied to the preparation of individual student IEP "goals and objectives" at a time when computerized "banks" of IEP goals and objectives had yet to be implemented. It was as if progress for students with disabilities could not veer from a basic, remedial approach. Or more to the point, as Heshusius observed, could do no more than to "force the innately unpredictable into the predictable, the unmeasurable into the measurable, and wholeness into fragmentation" (1982, p. 12).

2.4   *Making It Matter*

Such contradictions in practice became increasingly troubling the more I probed constructivism espoused by Heshusius, as it informed the Cambridge research project, and as it was enacted through my teaching with Logo. It became apparent that, as a professional, I was more accountable for bureaucratic compliance than I was for teaching students. Increasingly, I witnessed how special education had gotten it all wrong. I was intolerant of a system that gambled with the lives of young children and youths who were denied full access to an enriching curriculum; exasperated by the over-dependence on increasingly mindless mass-produced instructional materials; infuriated by the bloated bureaucracy that demanded increasingly greater amounts of teacher time to document compliance to regulations rather than to actually teach students; and enraged at programmatic protocols that all but dismissed teacher, student, and parent knowledge as worthy resources.[4] Taken together, this became my motivation to pursue a doctorate in special education, but always with the intention to expose its limits and imagine a better way forward.

3   Getting It All Wrong: Special Education, Reductionism, and a Mechanistic Worldview

Reductionism and positivism would prove too deeply embedded in policy, practice, and the devaluing of disability at the institutional level for easy displacement even as Heshusius' voice became stronger, in unison with contemporaries who decried the over-reliance of "objectivity-seeking" quantitative research on disability and in special education (Biklen & Bogdan, 1977; Blatt, 1972, 1984; Bogdan & Biklen, 1976; Bogdan & Taylor, 1977; Edgerton, 1967, 1970, 1975). These individuals authored the early research and scholarship that led to the birth of "critical special education" (Ware, 2004, 2005). Their calls for reform shaped the foundation needed to advance the field of disability studies in education (Connor, 2012; Mitchell, Snyder, & Ware, 2014; Ware, 2004, 2013, 2017). Their efforts to problematize special education as a bureaucratic system operating on multiple levels contributed to the elaboration of a multi-paradigmatic and multidisciplinary critique that remains the recognized starting point for disability studies in education—"before it had a name" as Steven Taylor reminded decades later (2006). Keeping in mind that Heshusius was integral to this pursuit, as the authors in this book reveal, readers today will find her work as vibrant and relevant today as it was decades ago. It would be fitting that, perhaps, her voice becomes even stronger as a new generation of scholars finds their way, through this book series, and to new ways to apply her research and scholarship today.

3.1 Allies in Alternative Research Paradigms

In the process of preparing for this book and discussing its relevance with Heshusius, she was quick to remind that she was inspired by another circle of like minds who were equally important allies, non–special education colleagues who presaged a shift to qualitative and interpretative research methods in educational research (Lincoln & Guba, 1985; Guba, 1989). She recalled the "Alternative Paradigms Conference," a small but pivotal conference held in San Francisco, organized by Egon Guba and co-sponsored by the School of Education at Indiana University and Phi Beta Kappa. The conference papers were published as "The Paradigm Dialog" (Guba, 1989), with an introduction that noted the purpose of the conference was "*not* to crown the new queen of paradigms, but to clarify the rival alternatives that have emerged" (1989, p. 9). Conference presenters tackled the hegemony of positivist research organized across three "emergent" paradigms: postpositivism, presented by Denis Phillips; critical theory, presented by Thomas Popkewitz; and constructivism, presented by Yvonna Lincoln. Eight issues were identified to generate debate and dialog: "Accomodation," "Ethics," "Goodness criteria," "Implementation," "Knowledge accumulation," "Methodology," "Training," and "Values." Included among the speakers, now recognized as the forerunners in advancing qualitative research, were John K. Smith, Thomas Schwandt, Shulamit Reinharz, and Patti Lather. The respondents included Catherine Marshall, Margaret LeCompte, Gail McCutcheon, Madeline Grumet, Thomas Skrtic, and Lous

BOREDOM, REFUSAL, AND DISBELIEF

Heshusius (the "Goodness criteria" discussant note-taker). Elliot Eisner and Samuel Peshkin were additional speakers at this small conference that served to legitimate the development of qualitative methods in educational research. Guba's edited collection became invaluable to many qualitative researchers and especially doctoral students who lacked access to mentors that might guide their research.

It should not go without notice that this same conference was described elsewhere by Gage (1989) as an event that might well signal the "demise of objectivity-seeking quantitative research on teaching—a victim of putatively devastating attacks from anti-naturalists, interpretivists, and critical theorists" (p. 4). Gage published a futuristic "history" of the "Paradigm Wars and Their Aftermath" (1989) in *The Educational Researcher*. He relied upon the rhetorical device of being one who has glimpsed into the future (2009) and realized that "the interpretivists' ethnographic studies flourished, enhancing the cultural appropriateness of schooling, and critical theorists' analyses fostered the struggles for power for the poor, non-Whites, and women" (p. 4). Fear fuelled the rage expressed by Gage, who actually failed to mention Heshusius by name, although she offered a powerful critique as a respondent during the actual conference. Although this was a small role in the conference, her words resonated among the growing number of interpretivist researchers who posed a threat to the exclusive reliance upon quantitative research in education. They formed the spine for launching a new focus for research located in the excavation of "immediate meanings of action from the actor's point of view" (Gage, 1989, citing Erikson, 1986).

Just to remind, it was in the early 1970s that Heshusius began her doctoral research—a participant observation of adults with mental retardation residing in a group home (Heshusius, 1978). As Heshusius probed the meaning these individuals made of their lives and learning from their lives, she realized the clear limits of positivist, quantitative research on disability for many reasons. Chief among them was the "virtual absence of the voices of the people most involved—the exceptional persons themselves" (1981, p. v). Heshusius noted that what seemed so obvious to those who might look closely, the "profound implications for program planning and further research if we decide to start listening to the persons we label incompetent" (1981, p. vii). Her work drew from many of the strongest advocates for qualitative research methods in disability-based research published in the 1970s and late 1960s, including Burton Blatt, Doug Biklen, Robert Bogdan, Ellen Brantlinger, Robert Edgerton, Steve Taylor, William Rhodes, and Wolf Wolfensberger. These scholars paved the way for Heshusius to continue to dissect positivism and to assert the value of interdisciplinary, multi-methods research methods in the study of disability in schools or society. Decades later, as Heshusius recalled her experience for this author, she reiterated the belief that there was a convergence of these two forces in her mind that propelled her thinking about the possibility for infusing an anti-positivist critique into special education practice and teacher preparation. Hers was a fresh, avant-garde approach to making meaningful connections for those who followed her work.

In the example of the concluding essay in the LDQ *Special Issue* titled, "Why Would They and I Want to Do It? A Phenomenological-Theoretical View of Special Education" (1984), Heshusius proved to be provocative on multiple levels. The title posed a bold and provocative question; the visual presentation of her text stood apart from the typical format for special education journals; and as a researcher, she melded past and present, teacher and student. Heshusius opened with a poem penned by a practitioner in response to an earlier publication by Heshusius, "At the Heart of the Advocacy Dilemma: A Mechanistic Worldview" (1982). That earlier work appeared in the flagship special education journal, *Exceptional Children (EC)*, with a readership drawn from rehabilitative, therapeutic, and educational professionals. As a speech therapist, the poet lamented her profession's mindless conformance to a "therapeutic model organized around the smallest unit of language" (Katz, cited in Heshusius, p. 363). Katz recalled a time when she really enjoyed her work and the value it gave to her life. However, she held that special education had—as a consequence of practice and policy directives—all but guaranteed the diminishment of children and the professionals who worked with them. Katz described her crisis of confidence[5] that followed on professional disillusionment and discontent, wondering: *"What is our part, my part?* [do I] *walk away, say OK, or feign conformity"* (1984, p. 19).

The poem served to position Heshusius' critique of institutions through an ever-reverent respect for the frontline workers who find themselves as unwitting collaborators propping up an unresponsive system. Years passed, before, as a doctoral student, that I met Heshusius. Though, not one known to gush, I was drawn to her compassion and interest in the practioner perspective I offered as I introduced myself. She recounted how frequently her writing prompted personal responses from individuals, especially teachers—a community for whom she felt particular empathy and understanding. Indeed, she possessed intricate and deep understanding of teachers' smallest joys, and of the dilemmas and futility that too often followed individual efforts to change practice beyond the walls of our classrooms. She offered no solutions per se, but instead encouraged special educators and related professionals to reflect upon their work and to name what they found troubling about practice. She included many such examples from her own experience to make this point in her 1984 LDQ article:

I remember looking at the drawers full of programmed materials, task-an-
alyzed tasks, phonic exercises, and remedial programs, all showing a
remarkable similarity: pieces of things. Filling in blanks. Filling in letters.
Word-attack skills for isolated words. Marking multiple-choice answers.
I would force myself to read it all, or rather not to read but to skim, for
there was nothing to really read. I would get lost, then, force myself to
start over again, and I would invariably feel a tiredness, a sudden fatigue.
I was not absorbing anything. My own mind had become a blank. Yet, I
would tell myself: I need to use them, for weren't others doing so, and
didn't all these publishers publish them, didn't theories support them,
didn't I see them in curriculum laboratories and at instructional materials exhibitions? I would think of the students I had to teach the next day,
and I would feel depressed, powerless, even desperate. (1984, p. 364)

For Heshusius, the process of naming all that she encountered as troubling in
her chosen profession ultimately gave her the strength to resist and the permission to teach unfettered by:

... remedial materials, perceptual deficits, task analysis, precision teaching, mastery learning, systemic stimulus control, token economies, systematic positive or negative reinforcement (I never understood the
difference since for me they were both negative), programmed and
sequenced and self-correcting materials, daily charting, behavioural
objectives, computerized or otherwise assembled, and the sixty-some
(or was it six hundred, or six thousand?) sequential steps to reading. We
started using regular library books again the students could freely choose,
did writing tasks that were of importance for their own living, developed
projects together, watched and talked about films, read the newspaper,
and wove into all of it the teaching of the needed concepts and the skills
in such a way that the students saw the skills as functional for their personal uses. (1984, p. 364)

4   Conclusion: Making Difference Matter in Spaces That Resist

Heshusius came to her insights informed by practice, close observation, and
meaningful engagement on and with disability in a time when ableism and
the critique of institutional ableism had yet to be named. On this, she never
wavered from her claims to advance a "non-mechanistic, holistic, participatory
view of knowledge in which facts, values, ethics, and meanings are no longer

artificially separated" (1984, p. 367). Writing today, nearly four decades later, it is interesting to note that although such a message was initially published in traditional special education publications and welcome in conference venues of professional organizations linked to the Council for Exceptional Children (CEC), it would be less welcome today. Once interest grew in the alternate paradigm dialogue, traditional positivist researchers reacted to extinguish access to Heshusius and others who gained momentum with their critique. To this day, I receive emails from newly minted Assistant professors who are troubled by the fact that their interest in alternative, multi-paradigmatic perspectives in special education. One recently hired assistant professor emailed her struggle just two months into her first appointment to seek advice, noting that: "it's as if they overlooked my disability studies focus—and that was the whole focus of my job talk" (personal correspondence).

Amid growing national and international interest in her work, Heshusius recalled that she too, met with criticism within her own department at a major research university. In our conversations over the years, she recalled one time when her special education colleagues spent the greater part of a faculty meeting "damning" her audacious and provocative writing (2004b, p. 175). Worried, perhaps, as many are today, that special education would not be able to deliver on its promise, the traditionalists often decried those who spoke out against the status quo. Throughout the academy—beyond the institution that employed Heshusius—outrage was expressed by traditional special educators in a public and hostile "take down" in the very pages of many of the same journals that once welcomed their work. Heshusius and many others stayed on point in the face of unscrupulous colleagues, which has set the stage for the many critical voices that would follow in their footsteps.

In closing, I want to underscore the need for a return to the entire content of the 1984 *LDQ Special Issue* as it remains as valuable for teachers today as it ever was over three decades ago. The articles were written in clear and concise language and easily accessible to the novice educators in my current undergraduate and graduate courses. Despite the initial impulse for some to wince at the perception of the reading as "dated" content, they are soon silenced as they read themselves into this work, whether as practicing teachers or as students immersed in pre-service teacher preparation coursework. Reading Heshusius today inspires new ways to think about disability as a tool to critique uninterrogated special education practice. In many ways, the field of special education remains much as it was early in the 1980s when the "alternative paradigm" critique emerged (Connor, 2012, 2018). However, what emerged from that early exchange is the robust field of disability studies that now provides K–12 educators with legitimate ways to know and more fully understand disability as an experience that need not be named a problem. It is this small but significant truth that underscores the incompatibility of the distinct paradigms that

BOREDOM, REFUSAL, AND DISBELIEF

inform special education and disability studies. Heshusius and others probed this small truth and made it easier to remind educators today that *Disability Studies is not Special Education.*

Notes

1 DISTAR is an acronym for Direct Instruction System for Teaching Arithmetic and Reading, informed by the research of two prominent American behaviorists, Siegfried Engleman and Wesley C. Becker, dating back to the mid-1960s. Techniques of operant conditioning were integrated into teaching and learning strategies that paved the way for rote/recall learning in a direct-instruction "strategies" approach to remediate low-performing students, many of whom were non-white (Engleman, 1968). As a pedagogical approach to learning rooted to reductionist and mechanistic thinking, many educational theorists argued that such an approach discouraged teacher and student creativity through conformity on heavily scripted instruction. Mary Poplin, Lous Heshusius, Richard Iano, and others challenged the lack of humanistic framing that DI/DISTAR endorsed, and that in turn led them to advance Holism (*LDQ*, 1984).

2 Chakraborty (2013) recently compiled a thorough review of the "recurring, contentious issue" issue of the "deskilling of the teacher profession." In discussion of literature that dates back to the 1970s, Chakraborty outlined prominent threads in the literature, citing increased bureaucratic mandates and the subsequent debilitating effect on teachers, in combination with centralizing regulatory processes and the commercial markets that drive education curriculum, and thus educational practice. This is a concise and compact offering of a complex and enduring phenomenon in teacher preparation programs world-wide.

3 My teacher-designed curriculum was featured in a Council for Exceptional Children (CEC) publication following on research into my teaching by Cambridge-based researchers at Technical Education Research Center (TERC), Cambridge, MA, and Educational (Russell et al., 1989). I was described as among "the first teachers in the country to explore the use of problem-solving software with special education students" (p. xiv).

4 These same themes were featured in my first peer-reviewed publication in *The Journal of Educational and Psychological Consultation—Contextual Barriers to Collaboration* (1994). This special issue was focused on the importance of collaboration in special education. I offered a counternarrative that detailed the "parody of collaboration" given the multiple obstacles created by unchecked power structures in K–12 schooling. It was only in the preparation of this chapter that I realized I had unwittingly mimicked Heshusius when I sought to open with the words of the feminist writer Tilly Olsen, from a passage in the short story "I Stand Here Ironing" (1953). The challenge this text block posed to the journal publishers (Lawrence Erlbaum and Associates) was an onerous battle that I ultimately lost. Unlike Heshusius, who

succeeded in 1984 to publish the poem by Katz with proper use of italics and indentation for line breaks, 10 years later I was not permitted to veer from the template for academic journals by inserting Olsen's opening paragraph. Instead Olsen's text was awkwardly positioned as if it were a part of my writing—no italics allowed. Little did I know then that such obstacles would prove to be the norm for those who attempted to veer from the thickly drawn lines to exclude interdisciplinary pursuits in special education—and the world of academic publishing.

5 Another volume in this series, *From Critical Special Education to Disability Studies in Education,* features the work of Thomas M. Skrtic, who described the experience recounted by Katz as a "crisis of confidence" resulting from doubt and uncertainty about one's professional work. This occurred in the face of deconstructing a paradigm which left an individual caught between the past preparation, the practice challenge of the present, and the uncertainty of the future. In more poetic phrasing, Katz noted "What is our part, my part?" Do I "walk away, say OK, or feign conformity."

References

Barton, L., & Tomlinson, S. (Eds.). (1984). *Special education and social interests.* London: Croom-Helm.

Biklen, D., & Bogdan, R. (1977). Media portrayals of disabled people: A study in stereotypes. *Interracial Books for Children Bulletin, 8*(6–7), 4–9.

Blatt, B. (1972). Public policy and the education of children with special needs. *Exceptional Children, 38*(7), 537–545.

Blatt, B. (1984). On distorting reality to comprehend distortion. *Journal of Learning Disabilities, 17,* 627–628.

Bogdan, R. (1982). The disabled: Media's monster. *Social Policy, 13*(2), 32–35.

Bogdan, R., & Biklen, D. (1977). Handicapism. *Social Policy, 7*(5), 14–19.

Bogdan, R., & Kuglemass, J. (1984). Case studies in mainstreaming: A symbolic interactionalists approach to special schooling. In L. Barton & S. Tomlinson (Eds.), *Special education and social interests* (pp. 173–191). New York, NY: Nichols.

Bogdan, R., & Taylor, S. (1976). The judged, not the judges: An insider's view of mental retardation. *American Psychologist, 31*(1), 47.

Chakraborty, S. (2013). Deskilling of the teaching profession. In J. Ainsworth (Ed.), *Sociology of education: An A-to-Z guide* (pp. 183–185). Newbury Park, CA: Sage.

Connor, D. J. (2012). *A history of disability studies in education* (webpage). Retrieved from http://www.hunter.cuny.edu/conferences/dse-2012/history-of-disability-studies-in-education

Connor, D. J. (2018). *Contemplating dis/ability in schools and society: A life in education.* New York, NY: Rowman & Littlefield.

Engleman, S. E. (1968). Relating operant techniques to programming and teaching. *Journal of School Psychology, 6,* 89–96.

Erickson, F. (1986). Qualitative methods in research on teaching. In M. C. Wittrock (Ed.), *Handbook of research on teaching* (3rd ed., pp. 119–161). New York, NY: Macmillan.

Gage, N. L. (1989). The paradigm wars and their aftermath: A "historical" sketch of research in teaching since 1989. *Educational Researcher, 18*(7), 4–10.

Gregory, A. (2017, August 20). The Cassandra effect: How the writer Rebecca Solnit became the unexpected voice of the resistance. *New York Times Magazine.* Retrieved from https://www.nytimes.com/2017/08/08/t-magazine/entertainment/rebecca-solnit-writer

Guba, E., & Lincoln, Y. S. (1988). *Fourth generation evaluation.* Newbury Park, CA: Sage.

Heshusius, L. (1982). At the heart of the advocacy dilemma: A mechanistic world view. *Exceptional Children, 49*(1), 6–13.

Heshusius, L. (1984). Why would they and I want to do it? A phenomenological-theoretical view of special education. *Learning Disabilities Quarterly, 7*(4), 363–368.

Heshusius, L. (2004a). Special education knowledges: The inevitable struggle with the "self." In L. Ware (Ed.), *Ideology and the politics of (in)exclusion* (pp. 143–165). New York, NY: Peter Lang.

Heshusius, L. (2004b). From creative discontent toward epistemological freedom in special education: Reflections on a 25-year journey. In D. J. Gallagher, L. Heshusius, R. P. Iano, & T. M. Skrtic (Eds.), *Challenging orthodoxy in special education: Dissenting voices* (pp. 169–230). Denver, CO: Love Publishing.

Lincoln, Y. S., & Guba, E. G. (1985). *Naturalistic inquiry.* Newbury Park, CA: Sage.

Mitchell, D. T., Snyder, S. L., & Ware, L. (2014). Curricular cripistemologies: Or every child left behind. *Journal of Literary and Cultural Disability Studies, 8*(3), 301–319.

Poplin, M. S. (1984). Toward a holistic view of persons with learning disabilities. *Learning Disabilities Quarterly, 7*(4), 290–294.

Russell, S. J., Corwin, R., Mokros, J. R., & Kapissovsky, P. M. (1989). *Beyond drill and practice: Expanding the computer mainstream.* Reston, VA: Council for Exceptional Children.

Skrtic, T. M. (1988). The crisis in special education knowledge. In E. L. Meyen & T. M. Skrtic (Eds.), *Exceptional children* (3rd ed.). Denver, CO: Love Publishing.

Ware, L. P. (1989). Problem-solving software. In S. J. Russell, R. Corwin, J. R. Mokros, & P. M. Kapissovsky (Eds.), *Beyond drill and practice: Expanding the computer mainstream.* Reston, VA: Council for Exceptional Children.

Ware, L. P. (1994). Contextual barriers to collaboration. *Journal of Educational and Psychological Consultation, 5*(4), 339–357.

Ware, L. P. (2004). *Ideology and the politics of (in)exclusion.* New York, NY: Peter Lang.

Ware, L. P. (2013). Special education teacher preparation: Growing disability studies in the absence of resistance. In G. Wilgus (Ed.), *Knowledge, pedagogy and postmulticulturalism: Shifting the locus of learning in urban teacher education* (pp. 153–176). New York, NY: Palgrave.

Ware, L. P. (2017). Disability studies in K–12 Education. In L. J. Davis (Ed.), *Beginning with disability: A primer* (pp. 257–305). New York, NY & London: Routledge.

CHAPTER 2

New to the "Family of Malcontents": Reflections on an Early Career of Creative Discontent

Emily A. Nusbaum

If you want to make a human being into a monster, deny them, at the cultural level, any reflection of themselves.

JUNOT DIAZ

∴

Abstracts

This chapter details the practice of special education's misguided ideology in the assessment and placement practices common to the IEP meeting. Nusbaum offers a nuanced account of her experience attempting to advocate for Lelia, a young student who could only be seen by professionals as an amalgam of deficiency and lack. Nusbaum provides an account that is richly textured by the insights Heshusius offered to the professional literature, decades before it was recognized for its merit.

Keywords

Individualized Education Plan – school psychologists – consultant advocate – advocacy dilemma – inclusion

In this chapter I use Heshusius' (1989, 2004) work to trace my entrance into doctoral work and academic life in disability studies, through a series of vignettes that represent various points of my professional development. Her notion of "paradigm-as-metaphor" describes the ways in which we view, understand, and experience the world as a metaphor, in and of itself. Through its use I articulate the questions that drove me to pursue doctoral work and continue

© KONINKLIJKE BRILL NV, LEIDEN, 2020 | DOI: 10.1163/9789004427280_003

to this day to frame my scholarly work and teaching. Her construct gives me the words to describe ways of experiencing the world that have separated me (and thus my thinking, writing, teaching, and ultimately *who* I am) from many of my colleagues in traditional, special education departments where I have worked over the years.

Similarly, Heshusius' (2004) discussion of "the inevitable struggle with the self," has proven to be a useful referent in many of my graduate, education courses, where I have documented the challenges of this approach in my work with practicing teachers and education professionals steeped in traditional, special education worlds. Heshusius' writing about participatory consciousness (Heshusius, 1994) became a reference guide to encourage pre/early-service teachers and other professionals as they considered ways to relate to disabled students—through a kind of connectedness, openness, and receptivity that Heshusius describes as a "total turning to the other" (citing Schachtnel, 1959, p. 225). My examples are drawn from work with pre/early-service teachers steeped in a framework of positivist thinking who experienced great difficulty understanding their own *self-other* construction.

That is, these teachers' inability to "self-forget" collided with their ability to relinquish the desire to "get it right" in an assignment to observe a student with disability. Later in the semester, course evaluations by some students reflect the challenge that many of them had with having what Heshusius describes as a "silent mind" and moving to a state of complete attention to "the other." Students' challenges with this assignment reflect their inability to summon the space that Fine (1994) describes as "working the hyphens," which describes the inner, deeply personal, somatic acts that stand between the researcher/researched and as I suggest here, many education professionals and their students.

1   Paradigm-as-Metaphor

Two experiences remain so acutely clear in my mind as the impetus for my pursuit of doctoral work. The first followed on my experience as an inclusion facilitator in a large, urban school district in northern California, which in turn, led to private consultant work with families in mediation and litigation against school districts. Families that I worked with wanted the opportunity for their children, labeled with disability and housed in segregated classes, to receive educational supports and services in the context of age-appropriate, general education classrooms. Both of the experiences detailed below involved Individual Education Plan (IEP) meetings attended by parents, a disability-rights attorney and me, as their consultant—staged with us huddled at one end of a large table—diminished in number by the multiple teachers, administrators, and attorneys representing a school district at the other end. IEP meetings often provide a unique context in which to manufacture student identity (Mehan, 1993; McDermott, 1993). Professionals often exert the muscle of "expertise" against families who are subjected to deficit-based narratives of their children based on the seemingly "objective" knowledge of these "experts."

I will describe two IEP meetings that are powerful representations of Heshusius' (1989) critique of the Newtonian Mechanistic paradigm that has largely shaped what "counts" as knowledge about disability in special education. Heshusius proposes a move from this epistemological privileging to "epistemological proprietorship" and reconsideration of what counts as knowledge and ownership via "epistemological possession" (Heshusius, 2004, p. 294). Her critique reminds us that the object of what is "known" only becomes known through the mechanistic/positivist acts of ranking and measuring. These insights are made self-evident in the exemplars that follow.

1.1   *Juan*

The first of these IEP meetings was with a family I had supported for over six years, during the time that their son was in late elementary and middle school. This family had attempted (unsuccessfully) to remove their son, Juan, from a segregated classroom into general education. At the IEP meeting, the family was fighting to block the recommendation that Juan be moved to a highly segregated facility for students labeled with intellectual disability. After six years of writing detailed reports that outlined the supports this young man needed and that further articulated school-wide practices that could support all students in general education, I made a gamble that felt short of my hopes and advocacy for Juan. I believed that presenting research—quantitative research—that documented the dismal life outcomes for individuals with disabilities educated in segregated settings, an evidence-based argument would persuade the school district team to recognize the injustice of banishing Juan to a segregated facility for his high school years. These were professionals who valued empirical data and evidence-based practice. He was constructed as "severely, mentally retarded" through the overreliance upon the quantification of assessment items that would yield a single number. His new identity was derived from standardized scores and age-equivalents that together reduced his humanness to the label of "severely mentally retarded."

After I presented the life-outcomes research, Juan's mom read a statement about her hopes for her son's life—a life that was based in community, that was based on his competence, and that assumed he could and would participate in the richness of the world outside an institutional school facility. The school district team shook their professional heads at her detailed descriptions of what she believed was a possible future for her son. They returned to their interpretation of Juan and reminded her that he had "significant mental retardation." In as much, he would need the kinds of things that their professional knowledge dictated he would.

I looked Juan's teacher in the eye, and asked him "Would you make this same decision for your own child? If you knew the life outcomes tied to education in such segregated places? Or if you had the same hopes that his mom does?" When his teacher looked at me in return and said "yes" I realized that the way I understood the world and the place of disability within it was distinctly different than his. It was not just a matter of inclusive education or not. But was a more profound difference about *who* I am, at my epistemological core. I had not read any of Heshusius' work at this time, yet I remember my visceral discomfort and my absolute inability to understand this teacher's "way of seeing" Juan (which was, in effect, a way of "not seeing" him; Heshusius, 1989, citing Lincoln & Guba, 1985, p. 15). Informed by my own paradigm-as-metaphor, the practice of marking Juan as, essentially a failure at full humanness was not congruent with how I live in the world. To quantify, to "objectively" measure another human's essence in order to claim knowing, one must accept the concrete idea of failure.

1.2 Leila

That same year I attended another IEP meeting for an eighth-grader named Leila—a young woman who was a student in a district that I served as a consultant. It was an appointment I acquired through the federal court as the result of a class action lawsuit. In this small, K-8 school district, students faced the overwhelming structural inequities commonly associated with under-resourced urban schools and corresponding social challenges in communities affected by poverty. This young woman, who I supported in a general education classroom, had a range of support needs, such as cortical blindness, seizures, and was learning to use her left elbow to operate switches and communication technology. She and her mother had experienced homelessness for most of her life. Yet now, as an eighth grader, Leila was an integral part of her school community—when she was absent her classmates asked where she was and if she was okay, friends in her class were learning to provide feeding support to her in the cafeteria, and when there was a substitute aide in the classroom students taught the aide how to recognize when Leila had the smallest of seizures.

At her IEP meeting, in addition to the school team, Leila's doctors from the seizure clinic at a major medical school nearby were in attendance. The school psychologist began his report through a similar deficiency discourse descriptor of "severe retardation," "blindness," and "significant hearing loss." This was the first time hearing loss had been discussed and when pressed about how he arrived at this designation, the school psychologist talked about Leila's lack of response to a standard hearing screening done with headphones. I tried to counter this by describing her unique embodiment and the way her body moved in response to the different vocalizations she made when friends met her at the bus versus when an aide told her it was time to go to the bathroom as she wheeled out of her classroom. I described her visible excitement when she heard the voice of her teacher come into her classroom each morning (I should add that many female students became excited when their teacher—a young man, fresh-from-college and his Teach for America training) arrived. The school psychologist then re-countered my descriptions with his assessments and scores that all ranked Leila as having age-equivalents in development to a child under one year old. Leila's mom talked about how she knew her daughter could hear her and understands her at home—but again these descriptions were discredited and not included in the public record of Leila's being in the world. Next came the doctors, who talked about seizures and brain waves and concluded that, by their graphs and measurement, Leila was "no more than a vegetable."

The doctors shared that they did not understand why a school district would provide the services and supports and efforts of so many for Leila whose human worth was never considered. They confirmed that sending her back to a more institutional setting would be fine. I offered a different perspective focused on what Leila added to her school community and what her friendship meant to the girls in her classroom. I talked about the fact that her absence was relevant to the people who cared for her when she had been absent. The doctors held firm to the contention that what made us human was brain functioning—measured in brain waves—which was very minimal for Leila. Once again, Leila's general education teacher and I tried to talk the doctors and school psychologist into understanding her humanness in very different measures—that her humanness was evident in others' care for and consideration of her, of what she contributed, and that her presence was missed when she was not there—it was a paradigm-as-metaphor that the other professionals and physicians at the meeting could not accept.

1.3   *Paradigmatic Forces in Special Education*

Years later, when I began my doctoral program I obtained a copy of Deborah Gallagher's book *Challenging Orthodoxy in Special Education* and I think I must have devoured it in a weekend and felt such relief! Reading Dr. Heshusius'

(1989) piece "The Newtonian Mechanistic Paradigm, Special Education, and Contours of Alternatives: An Overview" revealed the paradigmatic forces at play in far too many IEP meetings. To some of the educational professionals and doctors I had encountered, humanness *could* (and more importantly *should*) be measured in someone's brainwaves, in age-equivalent scores, and thus, in labels like "severe mental retardation" proved essential. Even more significant is what followed, as decisions are made about school placement, access to curriculum, and programmatic supports and services that are exclusively acceptable only for those deemed as not quite fully human as we are. In policy and practice, these decisions are disguised in and justified by numbers, scores, and labels. All of which, concomitantly, allow professionals to *not confront* their own preservation of self and the self-images that they have constructed.

For the first three years of my academic career I worked at a large, state university in central California. In my position I coordinated a special education credential program in the area of "moderate-severe disabilities" (as designated by the state educational code). In the region of the state where I worked very few disabled children have access to non-segregated settings. Students who have support needs like Leila's are in totally segregated, institutional-like centers from ages 3–22 and continue to live highly segregated lives as adults once they exit the school system. Students in these center-based schools are educated in "classrooms" that span a broad range of chronological ages, with no access to age-appropriate core curriculum, individualized augmented communication supports, or to non-disabled peers. In one site that I repeatedly witnessed high school aged students subjected to a morning circle time, in which the teacher opened each day with the calendar activity common to pre-school settings (*What is today? What was yesterday? What is tomorrow?*). Students were wheeled to the window to look outside in answer to the question "what is the weather today?" Besides the fact that none of these students had access to robust systems of communication, it didn't seem to occur to anyone working in the classroom that these students had spent the majority of their school lives involved in this same morning circle. And that, perhaps, as high-school students, there was something more interesting and age-appropriate that they should be engaged in.

Students labeled with "intellectual disability" in local districts were primarily educated in "functional skills" classrooms. Their curriculum math knowledge and literacy were not "functional skills" as daily schedules in these classrooms, which also began with "circle/calendar time, " focused on things like: learning community signs, "communication time" (when the speech therapist came), and daily preparation for Special Olympics (without access to general education PE). Perhaps because positivist measurement tools identified these students as slightly higher on a scale of humanness—closer in quantified intelligence to those using the assessment tools—many of these students were in segregated classrooms housed on public school district school sites. They only had proximity to others like them, the "regular," "fully human" students in general education were they permitted to do so.

Students labeled with autism could qualify for "autism inclusion" programs in local districts and were allowed to exit segregated, applied behavior analysis (ABA) programs after they had amassed enough successful "trials" to indicate their emergence into being fully human. Heshusius' (1989) critique of quantitative measure of learning has distinct parallels to the use of ABA/discrete-trial training for autistic students: "Objectification of knowing and of knowledge, additive and linear progress, quantification, right and wrong answers, mastery of learning, and lack of consideration for context, meaning, and personal purposes ... are both dictated by and justify mechanistic thinking" (p. 406). That is, when human behavior is quantified on a continuous scale, with cut points that sort individual into categories (such as success/failure, normal/disabled, right/wrong) what counts as knowledge is circumscribed (in Leila's case, her classmates' love and care that for her and the accompanying meaning that she brought into the classroom—and thus her humanness—was devoid from assessment, labels, and placement decisions).

The fallacy that applied behavior analysis and discrete trial training can be used as tools through which a student with autism can be "made" more human, and thus offered access to mainstream schooling experiences, seems so obvious to me. Do the professionals that structure these programs really believe that all the data that thousands of trial sessions over the course of student's life generates, truly demonstrates the achievement of a level of humanness in which autism is *less present*? Is it true, then, that the students who are labeled with intellectual disability and placed in "functional skills" classrooms, where they spend long days doing task-boxes in preparation for an adult life spent in a sheltered workshop, don't have quite the same level of innate "humanness," since they are not discrete-trialed all day at school (I have yet to meet a student in functional skills classrooms who has task-boxed their way out of possessing "significant intellectual disability")? The continuum marks humanness on one end, non-humaness on the other—reified by professionals who have grown numb to the denial of human rights to those who deemed "non-human."

My questions about the impossible space between the positivist paradigm and my own—a paradigm that is rooted to something more organic, fluid, and unfixed—created many uncomfortable conversations with colleagues who conformed to this positivist paradigm. How can various positivist methods be used to identify "disability," thus giving permission for some students to be separated, incarcerated, marginalized, and abused—and yet these same methods be used to also measure and identify when some of these students have become more human? If this positivist, mechanistic paradigm is so true, then shouldn't all students with disability labels have the chance to "earn" or "prove" their humanness and worth within it? Shouldn't the hallmarks, of the mechanistic, positivist paradigm preclude a student who is identified with disability being be able to successfully remove this cloak via these same methods? Heshusius (2004) offers some possible responses to my questions via her description of a "threefold denial" of the metaphors of the positivist paradigm:

1. The denial that the self of a human being is deeply involved in these measuring and ranking acts.
2. The denial that such self is shaped by forces of history in all its ideological manifestations.
3. The denial that this self also fundamentally shaped by self-protecting inner needs and images in actual interactions. (p. 295)

Heshusius' (2004) citation of Vanier (1999) aptly describes unacknowledged emotions that are at the root of exclusionary practices such as these: "... We are all so frightened of losing what is important for us, the things that give us life, security, and status" (p. 73). By this, Vanier means that to remain distant—to live in a paradigm that maintains the self/other construction—is to live with fear and with deeply grasped attachment to the images that we hold of ourselves. Considering this in light of Heshusius' (1989) concept of paradigm-as-metaphor, the mechanistic processes that are at the heart of the positivist paradigm enact and re-enact the self-other separation in ways that are both unconscious and habitual, as well as in ways that are seen as desirable and the hallmark of seemingly more "objective" work.

1.4 Paradigms and Privileging in the Academy

Efforts to explain the relationship between the mechanistic paradigm and the worth of individual students has been replayed for me many times over since starting my academic career. What bores deep into me when I hear my colleagues explain, "*And then there are the really, really low ones.*" Each time I struggle to respond as I recall so many jarring encounters in the past with colleagues that left me aggrieved, and later wondering how it followed that I was the one perceived as strident or extreme.

In my first academic position I was asked to work with a senior faculty member from school psychology on a cross-departmental project. In our introductory meeting she asked me about my background and those areas that my teaching and scholarship are focused on. I spoke about the ideology and practice of inclusive education, teachers' work in inclusive schools, and disability studies in education, which the areas that my work was focused on at the time. Without missing a beat, she clarified: "you don't mean the really, really low ones, do you?" When I asked her what she meant and she clarified that she was talking the "really, really severe kids" and inclusive education. I smiled and took off my glasses and gazed out the window behind her so that I didn't have to look at her in the eyes and couldn't see her all that clearly. Conscious of my emotions, I hoped for a neutral tone in my response, "Oh yeah, I mean all kids." Her eyes widened and with her head-shaking in disapproval—she reminded me of her established authority: decades as a faculty member at the university, her full schedule giving standard assessments to kids and identifying disability in a local district one day a week, her accumulated experience and thus knowledge entrenched in the very paradigm I hoped to question in my career. It was, it seemed, a sort of exponential use of the mechanistic paradigm— more accumulated years using quantitative, positivist methods clearly had/ have more value, more legitimacy—and thus stronger claims to knowledge than my own.

I am struck in conversations like these. How I am supposed to be the one who eases away from what is perceived to be an extreme position—that of wanting kids to be understood as equally human and educated together? Although, in my mind, this faculty member's statement was the equivalent to the racism of special education (Collins, 2013), I could not express this or respond to her in any way that would indicate that, for reasons that are twofold. First, when you hold the position that is not aligned with the dominant paradigm-as-metaphor, I believe that you represent that possibility that another's paradigm has reached its limitations. This is a difficult enough venture with a willing explorer of her/his own boundaries in. But nudge someone close to the edges of the metaphor they live in, without their willingness and desire, fear, exercised in many unpleasant ways, takes over. Second, I have slowly learned the futility of this (or, perhaps as an untenured faculty member, I have learned that it is more dangerous to my promotion and tenure than anything else); the paradigm that this senior faculty member lives in, understands disability within, and thus that has framed her career in are not just incompatible with, but diametrically opposed to, my own. This is now how I understand those colleagues who tell me that my ideas about inclusive education are "intense" or "extreme," and who try to counter my thinking about disability as a very natural part of our world with examples of disabled individuals who require separation, segregation, or similar forms of social/emotional disconnection.

NEW TO THE "FAMILY OF MALCONTENTS"

2   The Inevitalbe Struggle with the Self

Reading Heshusius' (2004) description of her colleague, who related the fear that students reported about the possibility of becoming disabled, I am reminded of some of my own students' reactions to an assignment that used an observational exercise to foster the process of self-forgetting, versus arriving at a specific conclusion about a student (such as a score or level of achievement). This class assignment was intended to foster a "silent mind," and in that silence learn to see what the self is "doing" (versus doing something—an assignment—something to "get right") (Heshusius, 2004). Although I suspect that many students in my classes experience discomfort (and, perhaps, fear) exploring the paradigm that I teach, the assignment described here prompted anger from many students. Subsequent course evaluations cited my "close-mindedness" in reference to this assignment Further, students' insistence that there was something to "get right" (beyond trying out some measure of reflexivity and moving outside of their "expert self," as it relates to the students whom they serve) demonstrates exactly the deliberate and "separative" (Heshusius, 2004, p. 288) stance from which most of them approach their work.

2.1   *"Doing" Observation—A Class Assignment*

The assignment required five weeks of ongoing observation, writing, and reflecting, in response to a set of questions/considerations one of their own students. Each week had a different, guiding focus: meaningful relationships, power and control, things to look forward to, a sense of value and self-worth, and relevant skills and knowledge for a range of contexts/environments.[1] I talked with students in my class about awareness of their expert, knowing, professional selves and acknowledgement of the filter that this can bring to the observational exercise. We practiced reflexive work with one another through writing and discussion about "critical incidents" they experienced in their classrooms and that I experienced in my own teaching (Tripp, 1993). I also attempted to emphasize the importance of the "doing" of the observations—without arriving at a score, a goal, or an objective about or for one of their students—that the assignment is largely about bringing awareness to their "self-in-action" (p. 290) as it relates to work with disabled students, and articulating the ways-of-knowing about their students and to which teachers tightly grasp

My purpose in this assignment was to foster some sense of *participatory consciousness,* as described by Heshusius (1994). In her paper, Hesushius described participatory consciousness as an alternative to the dominance of both positive thought, as well as qualitative research that worked to "manage" one's subjectivity. The management of subjectivity, she argued, continued a separation of the "knower" from the "known" as a self-protective measure to maintain the privileged self, which upholds self-other constructions. Further, the management of subjectivity reifies power inequities, by maintaining distance between the knower and the known. Participatory consciousness, however, is described by Heshusius as a deep level of connectedness between the knower and the known: it is not a "method," per se, but rather a way of being in the world. She cites Schachtel's (1959) concept of "allocentric knowing" as a total openness, receptivity, and a "total turning to" (p. 225) to the other. My attempts to support students in practicing more complete attentiveness and listening as a way to set aside the separative impulses that are often at the core of educational research and teaching work, with the belief that one cannot protect the needs of the inner self—and also listen and be with another fully—at the same time.

2.2 *Reflecting as the Instructor*

In reflection on my own practice, I almost laugh now when I consider my earlier idealism and naiveté when making this assignment. Given the dominant practices in special education/teacher education that focus on skills that include lesson planning, classroom management, systematic instruction (task analysis), and assessment (standardized, quantitative tools designed to articulate "how much" disability students have are pervasive) how could I believe that following just one assignment, teachers would experience and understand deep, participatory knowing as complex and transformative? More to the point, when I consider the working contexts of the teachers in my course and how separate school structures (like segregated classrooms) further serve to reify and maintain "seperativeness" as a "reiterating process between the self and the other ... (that is) not something that already exists, but rather an agential construct that achieves separation each time again" (Heshusius, 1994, p. 147). In the dominant paradigm-as-metaphor in traditional special education separativeness is not only upheld, but is understood as the only option.

In further reflection, I realized that the inherent limitations of quantitative teaching evaluations would surely fail to capture my attempts to foster deep connection between students and teachers. Some comments on anonymous student evaluations from this course reflect the discomfort experienced by many early-service teachers in the class. Many pointed to the difficulty of engaging in an observational practice that would result in reflection on both one's own teaching practices and classroom structures (versus a student score or label), and more pointedly about the self within one's work. The exercise itself pushed against the boundaries of individual teachers' paradigms and ways of knowing their students. One student commented: "Emily doesn't let us have our own opinions about our students and assessment and instruction ... this class made me feel bad." For this student, moving outside her expert-self and being present in discomfort (similar to the "fear" described by Heshusius, 2004) was not possible. This teacher gave me ratings of 1/5 (1 being "poor") in the areas of: "the instructor gave assignments that were beneficial" and "I learned a great deal in this class."

Another comment from a course evaluation was: "this class has been very hard for me ... how to get the all the points for this assignment was not totally clear ... I hated not knowing how to get all of the points.[2]" What bears attention here is that the need for this teacher to "get something right" in this observational assignment was aligned with her own paradigm-as-metaphor, and as such, it actually prevented her from accessing the underlying purpose in the assignment—to engage in the process of self-forgetting. It is important to note that this same teacher rated me with 1/5 (in the areas of "providing opportunities to reflect on course content" and "providing opportunities to reflect on practice"), which were exactly the objectives of the observational exercises. Although I thought at the time, and do still today, that my scoring guidelines (see Note 3) for the observational exercise are clear, this student's comments reflect what Heshusius (1989) described as "accusations of fuzziness" from my students[3] and the implication that "if you cannot know mechanistically, you cannot know" (p. 408).

In my current academic position I primarily teach doctoral courses with practicing special education teachers and administrators who are also unfamiliar with the post-positivist/post-modern exercise of deconstruction (Skrtic, 1995). My students often cling to the systems of knowing that have served them well, yet few have willingly investigated the limits of the foundations of these paradigms. Like Heshusius (1994), I have found that this process is not personal enough—it does not get at the fears that are in the very present moment of actual encounters between individuals (like some of the ones that I have described in my experiences here). As Heshuisus (2004) indicates,

> [F]ears are operative in the present moment of actual encounters, not in the theoretical reflexivity about representation, language, and power— an important reflexivity, to be sure, but a reflexivity ... that does not call attention to the feelings, fears, and images of one's own self-in-action. (p. 149)

Without this examination of the inner, embodied self, uncovering forms of structural and institutional forms of oppression remains a detached an impersonal act, with my students exerting effort to uphold the idealized self that many of them cling to tightly.There are important parallels to Brantlinger's early (1997) critique of the emergence of inclusive education, and the "special"/"regular" education binary. Brantlinger's critique is centered on the preservation of the "regular" student in school specifically through the "disabled other," who is not ready to occupy the same spaces/locations as a "regular" student—specifically because their "otherness" upholds both the notion of the "regular" and also justifies the subsequent segregation of the other. For inclusive education to fully emerge, the understanding of self-in-action, requires a shift in consciousness—of "seeing inside," or "seeing the inner and outer as one" (p. 303), and it is deeply about "transformation of the self" (Nusbaum, Dickens, & Reamy, 2016).

It is here that I want to end by positioning this shift in consciousness and "seeing the inner and outer as one" (Heshusius, 2004, p. 303) as the place where I now focus most of my teaching and research efforts. I believe there is a more delicate deliberation to structuring my courses to require students to engage with the self-in-action (whether through practitioner-focused questions or in a research methods course) and with the hope that these opportunities will allow students to "see" the edges of the paradigms they live within as habitual and unconscious locations. Although I still struggle to make sense of and attempt to change a profession that marginalizes the very people it claims to serve, Heshusius' writing about the deep level of connectedness between the knower and the known anchors my belief in connectedness, openness, and receptivity—whereby each has the potential to heal, sustain, and nourish our relationships, professional work, experiences in schools, and our lives.

Notes

1 These writing prompts and the structure of this part of my course were developed with support from Susan Baglieri and her colleagues at Long Island University, based on methods of observing, describing, and reflecting from The Prospect Center.

2 This assignment was worth 50 points total; 10 points for each observation. Teachers received all points if their observational recording showed that they were: willing to reflect on their own stance, not make assumptions or judgments, and arrive at some new way-of-knowing about their students. There was no "correct" or "incorrect" completion of the observations beyond these guidelines. We talked through and looked at examples of this kind of observation based on The Prospect Center Method.

3 There were also very positive comments about new understandings, the ability to be reflective, the new subject knowledge, and my encouragement and availability to students. Scores on these evaluations were quite high: 4's and 5's on a 5 point scale.

References

Brantlinger, E. (1997). Using ideology: Cases of nonrecognition of the politics of research and practice in special education. *Review of Educational Research, 67*(4), 425–459. Retrieved from http://www.jstor.org/stable/1170517

Collins, K. (2013). *Ability profiling and school failure: One child's struggle to be seen as competent* (2nd ed.). New York, NY: Routledge.

Fine, M. (1994). Working the hyphens: Reinventing self and other in qualitative research. In N. K. Denzin & Y. S. Lincoln (Eds.), *Handbook of qualitative research* (pp. 70–82). Thousand Oaks, CA: Sage.

Heshusius, L. (1989). The Newtonian mechanistic paradigm, special education, and contours of alternatives: An overview. *Journal of Learning Disabilities, 22*(1), 403–415.

Heshusius, L. (1994). Freeing ourselves from objectivity: Managing subjectivity or turning toward a participatory mode of consciousness. *Educational Researcher, 23*(3), 15–22. Retrieved from http://www.jstor.org/stable/1177221

Heshusius, L. (2004). Special education knowledges: The inevitable struggle with the "self." In L. Ware (Ed.), *Ideology and the politics of (in)exclusion* (pp. 143–165). New York, NY: Peter Lang.

Lincoln, Y. S., & Guba, E. G. (1985). *Naturalistic inquiry*. Newberry Park, CA: Sage.

McDermott, R. P. (1993). Acquisition of a child by a learning disability: Understanding practice: Perspectives on activity and context. In S. Chaiklen & J. Lave (Eds.), *Understanding practice* (pp. 269–305). New York, NY: Oxford University Press.

Mehan, H. (1993). Beneath the skin and between the ears: A case study in the politics of representation. In S. Chaiklen & J. Lave (Eds.), *Understanding practice: Perspectives on activity and context* (pp. 241–268). New York, NY: Oxford University Press.

Skrtic, T. (1995). *Disability and democracy: Reconstructing (special) education for postmodernity*. New York, NY: Teachers College Press.

Tripp, D. (1993). *Critical incidents in teaching*. London: Routledge.

CHAPTER 3

Seeking the Real in an Unreal World on Reading Lous Heshusius

Alicia A. Broderick

Abstract

This chapter provides a further close rendering of "epistemological incongruence" set within the author's early years as a behavioral consultant supporting a young student with autism. Although trained and versed in Applied Behavior Analysis (ABA), Broderick fought the over-reliance on ABA for students with autism as the sure-fit solution to diminish problematic behaviors. Her struggle is conveyed in near poetic terms, in much the same way that Heshusius draws on the vocabulary of a strong poet.

Keywords

positivism – interpretivism – autism – advocacy – reflective practice – ideology

1   Introduction

In the late1990s, at a pivotal moment in the conceptualization of my dissertation inquiry, I happened upon the collaborative work of Lous Heshusius and Keith Ballard (1996) in their text, *From Positivism to Interpretivism and Beyond: Tales of Transformation in Educational & Social Research* [*The Mind-Body Connection*]. I have come to liken my own experiences in the world at that time with having fallen down the rabbit-hole with Alice. Fortunately, there at the bottom of that epistemological rabbit-hole, I found Lous Heshusius' work. In this chapter I explore the enduring impact of Heshusius' paradigmatic critiques in my own life by reflecting upon what she refers to as "life, real and unreal" (Heshusius, 1996a, p. 50). After exploring the ways in which her paradigmatic critiques first gave me a conceptual vocabulary for understanding my early career experiences with epistemological incongruence, I continue by exploring the layers of that early work that I didn't fully appreciate upon

© KONINKLIJKE BRILL NV, LEIDEN, 2020 | DOI: 10.1163/9789004427280_004

first reading of it, layers that continue to support me through my more current ontological travails, in part by exploring what might (and must) lie *beyond* interpretivism, as Heshusius and Ballard presaged in their text's title, *From Positivism to Interpretivism and Beyond*.

2 From Positivism to Interpretivism: Naming Epistemological Incongruence

2.1 *Early Career Experience*

In the 1990s, I was hired as an educational consultant for the family of a preschool aged boy who had just been labeled with autism. At the time of my hire the family had already begun a home program of 40 hours per week of discrete trial training based on principles of Applied Behavior Analysis and modeled largely after Lovaas's Young Autism Project. The child, whom I will refer to as Tommy, was drilled daily in programs aiming to teach such things as "non-verbal imitation," "eye contact," "following one-step verbal instructions" (compliance), and "basic play skills." As an inclusive preschool educator, I was charged with expanding the repertoire of "play" programs in Tommy's training, as he had been assessed to have no conventional independent play skills. While I experienced a rather unsettling sense of ambivalence with the task placed before me, I interpreted this at the time to be my own fear that I might somehow not "measure up" to the task demands, and that my own status as "expert" might thus be compromised. I was not yet able to articulate my growing conviction that "play" could not be taught in a systematized, step-by-step manner, and I agreed to write several "play programs" for Tommy.

2.2 *Discrete Trials, Task Analysis, and My Failure to Follow the Play Regime*

Day after day passed, and I wrote nothing. I played with Tommy every day, alternating between conducting the formal discrete trial programs already in place, and getting down on the floor and playing with him. I followed his lead, seizing on any interaction he initiated with toys (including banging on them and throwing them), and I imitated him. When I had his attention, I modeled a particular way of interacting with the toy—pushing a button, pulling a lever, spinning a bead—and facilitated his interaction with the toy in a similar way. I used no linear or hierarchical system of "fading" as was the case in the discrete trial programs, e.g., moving from physical prompt to gestural prompt to verbal prompt; nor did I stop to record with a check mark each time I adjusted my support. Sometimes that support consisted of my guiding his hand through an entire movement, and sometimes of my "hovering" over his hand through the movement, alternating between providing a guiding touch and letting go, encouraging him to continue with the movement on his own. I sought his attention by surprising him, with silly and unexpected things one could do with toys. Sometimes I merely touched the button or lever and touched his elbow, waiting for him to try it on his own, but moving in to support the movement if necessary. I utterly failed to partition our play into anything even vaguely resembling "discrete trials," and came to think of our interactions around play as characterized by a growing sense of fluidity, complexity, spontaneity and creativity.

Fewer than 3 weeks later, Tommy had begun to independently approach and initiate play with several different toddler cause and effect toys (pop-up toys, bead mazes, shape sorters, etc.). Pleased with his expanding play, Tommy's mother looked in his program book to see what the data on his play programs looked like. She quickly discovered that I had not written any new play programs, and asked me what I had been doing with him. I explained how difficult I found it to systematize a step-by-step procedure for learning to play, and I tried to explain the many different interactive ways I had been supporting his emerging play. Tommy's mother listened to me with strained politeness, and shared her conviction that anything—including play—could be task analyzed and written up in terms of discrete, sequential behavioral objectives.

I protested, saying that I didn't think that activities such as playing with a shape sorter or a bead maze or a puzzle could be task analyzed. I tried to explain that I considered play to be a very dynamic and fluid activity. The ways that I supported Tommy when we played depended on what he did from moment to moment in our interaction—I responded to him and he responded to me.

2.3 The Data Mandate—"You Can Do It If You Try!"

Tommy's mother responded with encouragement, insisting that I could do it if I tried. She suggested that I simply try writing down exactly what I did with Tommy, acknowledging that this may feel somewhat artificial to me, but reassuring me that it could be done. She reminded me that all of the "empirical" research indicated that this was the best method of instruction for kids like Tommy. She stressed to me the importance to her of collecting data on discrete behavioral programs, because without that data, she had no way of knowing what Tommy was learning or how he was learning it. She also stressed to me that in order to secure monies from the school district to fund Tommy's home-based behavioral program, she needed to have the data to document that his home program was "working" and was an appropriate education for Tommy.

With some urgency in her voice, she told me that we had just lost 2–3 weeks of data, and she reminded me that she needed to see that data in order to know and to document that Tommy was learning.

I pointed to her son who sat on the floor not 10 feet away, turning the dial and pulling the handle on a See-n-Say toy. I gently suggested to her, "There's your data," and pointed out that he was playing with a toy on his own, something he hadn't been doing several weeks ago. I tried to explain that I didn't know what he was learning by looking at the program data; I knew what he was learning by playing with him and by carefully observing his play. She shook her head firmly, insisting that such "subjective" assessments were not helpful to her son, as only "empirical" (i.e., "quantitative") data would reliably indicate that he was learning specific skills as a direct result of specific teaching methods. Additionally, she stressed how important it was to her that I write down these play programs for Tommy, as I was only working with him on a temporary basis. After I left, she wanted the other therapists to be able to consistently replicate whatever I was doing that was working in my play interactions with Tommy.

As a professional, I felt deeply torn at her repeated request and wanting very much to meet the needs of Tommy and his family as I had been hired to do, but feeling as though I were somehow betraying my own sense of professional integrity by attempting to do so in this particular manner. Not fully understanding the source of this ambivalence, I agreed to make an attempt, but I continued to resist the idea of writing task analyses of play. Sensing that our disagreements ran far deeper than mere differences of opinion on instructional method, Tommy's mother and I mutually agreed to disagree.

Unfortunately, in my woefully inadequate and inarticulate plea to think of playing and learning in a different way, I believe the only thing I managed to convince Tommy's mother was my own professional inadequacy to perform the task she had hired me to do. As I understood it, the very nature of play was spontaneous, creative, and interactive—entirely antithetical to the prescribed, routinized, and reactive behavioral model I was being asked to force it into. However, I *had* been professionally trained and socialized within that behavioral framework myself, and I knew very well how to use the discourse of ABA and how to write and implement discrete instructional trials. I knew exactly what she wanted me to do—I had done it a hundred times before, but it no longer felt right to me. I was experiencing a growing sense of unease and profound doubt about what I thought I knew, and I felt myself grasping for a language to talk about it in any other way. What I knew—how to engage a child in play and in learning—seemed somehow not to count in this interaction; it was dismissed, disqualified as illegitimate knowledge.

3 Epistemological Shifts

Heshusius and Ballard (1996) place epistemological shifts such as the one I experienced squarely in the context of broader shifts in intellectual paradigms. While these authors began their collective inquiry as an exploration of experiences with shifting and alternative epistemologies, they report that contributing authors in their edited volume, nearly always reported similar epistemological shifts as preceding an accompanying shift in broader intellectual paradigm, specifically, the shift from "a quantitative, positivist epistemological framework to a qualitative, interpretive one," a shift that involves a "fundamental deconstruction and reconstruction of agreements about what counts as real and how we allow each other to claim knowledge" (p. 2). For Heshusuis and Ballard both, this shift in paradigmatic assumptions was not consciously embarked upon, nor was it brought about by any "systematically carried out intellectual pursuit" (p. 2). Rather:

> When we started to consciously reflect on how we had changed our most basic beliefs, we had to acknowledge that we knew, before we could account for it intellectually, that we no longer believed in what we were doing or in what we were being taught. (p. 2)

The way of knowing described by Heshusius and Ballard—knowing "before we could account for it intellectually"—was not unlike my own experience of *knowing* how to facilitate Tommy's play and *knowing* that there was an incongruence between that way of knowing and the language I had at my disposal to articulate what I knew. Although I was unable at the time to articulate the source of my ambivalence, I came to understand it as an epistemological incongruence, which was itself part of the larger process of my own paradigmatic transition from positivism to interpretivism in my thinking—not just about play, or teaching, or learning, but fundamentally about the ways in which we come to know and construct the world.

3.1 *From Positivism to Interpretivism*

When I first read this body of work, I perceived in it an undercurrent of cautiously celebratory optimism throughout that I found reassuring, comforting, heartening to read. I was not alone. The dominant positivist worldview (within [special] educational research) simply failed to recognize and appreciate my *way of knowing*. I was experiencing epistemological dissonance, incongruence. However, I wish I could say now, with what I perceived as Heshusius' confidence then, that "we no longer are forced to pretend that the unreal life is real"

SEEKING THE REAL IN AN UNREAL WORLD

(1996a, p. 55). Whence came Heshusius' optimism, her joy, her "loving [of] the journey, however difficult it has been" (1996a, p. 54)? Whence came her strength in the face of the epistemological violence about which she so powerfully wrote? That strength, that optimism, both of which I was so grateful to have encountered in her work in the late 1990s, have now become, and thus far remain, elusive to me.

In the last several years, I have once again found myself experiencing a disconcerting period of disequilibrium, much as I did in the mid-1990s when I first found solace in Heshusius' work. However, I have come to understand my current state of dissonance as stemming in part from attempts to live and work within and to communicate across deep and cavernous divides that I no longer experience as merely epistemological. I now apprehend the deeper layer of what Heshusius and Ballard were writing about—for paradigmatic shifts involve not merely conflicts over what counts as knowledge and how we claim to know, but further involve "fundamental deconstruction and reconstruction of agreements about what counts as real" (p. 2). That is, I have now come to conceptualize many of my dissonant experiences with the world as *ontological* incongruence, and moreover, as ontological violence and assault. And while Tommy was one of my companions during the early stages of my epistemological journey, my key companion during my more recent ontological journey has been my son, Nicholas, and once again, Lous Heshusius has silently and supportively walked alongside us as well.

4   Speaking Truth to Power: Naming Ontological Violence

In preparation for writing an early draft of this chapter, I read several passages of Heshusius' work aloud to my son, Nicky, who now unschools (Holt, 1976) at home. He is now thirteen years old, and is currently in his fifth year of post-public school liberation. However, he was in his second year of unschooling at home when I first read to him these passages from Heshusius' work. Leaving the public school system had been a difficult process for all of us, and throughout it I once again found myself doubting not merely what I knew or the legitimacy of what I thought I knew, but more insidiously, doubting the reality and the truth of my son's lived experience. So of course, I pulled out some of Lous' work, and began reading aloud to my son. Among the passages I read to him were these:

> Children still know in an embodied way, relying on their somatic and affective knowing as a primary source of information. Penny Oldfather

(1991, p. 181) spent a year in a 5th grade classroom listening to children talk about what turns them on or turns them off in their learning. The following conversation occurred when she asked a student how he felt when he was asked by his teacher to do something he could not do or disliked doing.

> Joe: My whole body feels like I want to throw up or something if I don't like something ... I mean I feel sick ... my body feels completely wrong. (Heshusius & Ballard, 1996, p. 3)

And this vivid description of what happened to Heshusius upon taking her first special education teaching position at an American school:

> I could not believe the drawers full of "stuff" that were handed to me. Loads of programmed materials, workbooks, worksheets, filling-in-the-blank exercises, phonics exercises, all sharing one overwhelming characteristic: They were pieces of things. Pieces without any context, without any meaning. Unreal. This piecemeal approach to teaching and learning literally drove me just about out of my mind. Again, my memory of this confrontation is an intensely bodily one: It was as if my heart sank into my stomach every time I tried to work with this "stuff." I would literally feel the pull of gravity and would feel a wave of something close to nausea go through me. (Heshusius, 1996a, p. 53)

My son's response to these passages was one of rapture—he literally leapt off the couch, knocking down several of my precariously piled stacks of books on the coffee table in the process, dancing around the room and shouting gleefully, "Someone understands, yes! Someone *actually* understands!" He then paused and looked at me somewhat more suspiciously and asked, "Are you sure she's a teacher?"

After reading the passages above from Lous' work, I asked Nicky what his body felt like when he was in school. This is what he said:

> I definitely felt like I was about to faint, I was about to throw up, and I also felt a stronger feeling of need for revenge than I have ever felt before. My heart seemed to stop beating; I felt like I had a heart attack. I felt like I was being hanged. I felt overwhelmed. I tried to shut off all my feelings but I often ended up being escorted out of the classroom leaving a foot of saltwater in the classroom—at least, it felt like that. In school I felt like I was being treated as a slave; they tried to herd us into slavery like cows

ready to be made into hamburger or something. I could never really enjoy lunch, because it felt like the last meal that a prisoner would have before hanging. In school, I sometimes managed to shut off myself, sort of like a robot, but that's not the real me.

Listening to Nicky's testimony about his somatic experience of schooling was difficult for me then and remains difficult now; his discomfort was real and it was total—physically, intellectually, and emotionally. Consistent with Heshusius' testimony of her experiences, Nicky's epistemological incongruence was also an intensely somatic experience—knowing "in an embodied way, relying on ... somatic and affective knowing as a primary source of information" (Heshusius & Ballard, 1996, p. 3). Yet perhaps the most disturbing piece of this for me as his mother to hear was finally realizing the extent to which he resorted to disassociation from his own body and feelings—his own person—in an attempt to cope with the incongruence between what he *knew and experienced* about schooling and the narratives he was being told in school. Consistent with Heshusius' testimony, the somatic experience of his epistemological incongruence was dissonant, aversive, and deeply unpleasant—experienced as anxiety, faintness, nausea, "like I had a heart attack," "like I was being hanged"—so deeply unpleasant that "I tried to shut off all my feelings," "sort of like a robot," a coping mechanism that ultimately (and thankfully), failed.

5 Rules, Boundararies, Routines and Rituals

My son courageously objected to his very first experience of schooling in ways that continued for years to shape his opinion of schools: On his very first day of preschool (his teacher told me some months later), she felt it necessary to send a child to the "time out chair"—it was her very first day as a preschool teacher, and someone in her teacher preparation had no doubt encouraged her to establish such "rules" and "boundaries" and "routines" from the very beginning. My son had never heard of nor apparently conceived of anything like a time out chair, and when she sent the child seated next to him (whom he had met that very afternoon) to "do his time" in the forced exclusion from the circle for some minor infraction, the child dutifully walked over to serve his sentence. Nicky apparently found this notion preposterous, and he followed the child to the chair, pulled up another chair alongside him and sat down, silently putting his arm around the child's shoulders. His teacher asked Nicky to return to the rug. "No," he said. "You're taking his freedom away, and that's unkind. If he's going to have no freedom, at least he won't be lonely." She told me that she did not force him to return to the circle, and that the boys returned together when the requisite sentence had been served. By mid-year, the time-out chair had disappeared from her classroom and by the time my daughter entered her classroom 4 years later, she appeared not to use exclusion in any systematic way as a strategy for inducing compliance among children. And ten years later, this child who was sent to the time-out chair on the first day of Pre-K continues to be one of Nicky's closest friends, despite the fact that they no longer attend school together and have each grown into very different children with different interests and circles of friends.

For years, Nicky continued to resist the rituals of schooling on a daily basis, but after his early acts of active resistance, eventually fell into a daily pattern of the somewhat more passive resistance of the survivor. Not one single day in his life did he willingly go to school. The most horrifying part of this ritual betrayal that we performed daily (and for years) was the passivity with which he ultimately squelched his own resistance and acquiesced. He never spoke a single word in the morning while getting ready for school, and although he would not actively participate in this ritual by dressing himself, he nevertheless permitted us to dress him and to feed him, as one might a doll. He allowed us to take him by the hand, and he walked with leaden feet, "sort of like a robot," as we led him to the school building each morning. And each morning he looked up at us with the same stricken expression of betrayal on his face, as he compliantly walked into the building, pleading silently with his eyes, "How can you do this to me?" And every single day, he was surprised anew by our betrayal.

About a year before we finally pulled Nicky out of school and brought him home to learn, I recall sitting on the front steps of his elementary school one summer evening, after having passed a pleasant evening playing on the playground with the neighborhood children. We sat on the front stoop of the building to rest, and he looked wistfully up at it with a sadness on his face that had come to be all too familiar to me. Nevertheless, I persisted in asking, "What are you thinking?" to which he responded, "look at it." I did—it was a somewhat dilapidated red brick colonial building, built in 1931, complete with a white-painted cupola with columns and a copper-plated dome and weather vane. At the foot of the front steps, we sat in its imposing shadow. His eyes misted over as he went on, "I feel bad for it. It should be a proud place, but it can't be. They tell too many lies in there."

My son, from a very early age, has experienced schooling not just as epistemological incongruence, but apparently, also as ontological assault. Schooling not only denied his ways of knowing, but asserted ontological claims that he knew and understood to be "lies," thus calling his lived reality into question on a daily basis. Valente (2011) refers to a similar phenomenon often experienced by Deaf students in hearing schools as "epistemic violence" (p. 35), and

SEEKING THE REAL IN AN UNREAL WORLD

argues that "Epistemically violent phonocentrism/audism [and, more broadly, ableism] works to (de)humanize, (ab)normalize, and discipline the always already failing body" (p. 67). While I find the notion of epistemic violence useful for understanding and making sense of my son's experience, I now maintain that the violence my son experienced is *more* than epistemic, and that the assault experienced is also ontological, undermining not merely how one knows but also what one perceives to be real. My son knows with his gut, and is not mystified by the constant barrage in contemporary public schooling of ontological assertions that counter what he knows to be real. As Heshusius and Ballard (1996) remind us, "Children still know in an embodied way, relying on their somatic and affective knowing as a primary source of information" (p. 3). For example, he did not accept the logic of social exclusion as a justified and earned response to a minor behavioral infraction, but named it, consistent with his material ontology, as "taking [a child's] freedom away." And while at times he "tried to shut off all [his] feelings," "sort of like a robot," he nevertheless continued to reassert the legitimacy of his lived reality through making counternarrative claims to the dominant narratives of schooling. He alternately made sense of the ontological dissonance at times by subjugating his own reality, but at other times by asserting, "they tell too many lies in there."

In reflecting upon his continued and repeated assertions of his own ontological experience, I am reminded of Heshusius' (1996a) discussion of her first class in graduate school wherein she found a professor lecturing about rats, rather than children:

> I still vividly remember being dazed. I remember it as if it happened yesterday. The shock to my entire system was too great to ever forget ... Something was WRONG! I felt it, not as an intellectual analysis (which was not available to me at the time), but as a bodily/somatic experience: I was stunned. I could not follow what was going on. While everyone seemed busy taking notes, I sat there feeling completely isolated and confused. I remember having difficulty getting up from my seat at the end of class. My mind kept saying: This is not about education. What am I doing here? Yet everyone else around me seemed to act normal, as if nothing were wrong. (p. 51)

As I reread this passage now, years after having read it for the first time, I cannot help but imagine my own son sitting, dazed and stunned, in a public school classroom, thinking "This is not about education. What am I doing here?" And yet the discursive practices of schooling go merrily along around him, and everyone else seems to act normal, as if nothing were wrong.

6 "We Can Include Him"; Disablement as a Prerequisite to "Inclusion"

Fast forward five years from the Pre-K scenario: I will never forget sitting, with my husband, across the table from our son's principal when he assured us, "We can include him" in reference to our son. My blood ran cold, my fists clenched, my eyes narrowed, and I reared into full Mama Lion protection mode. He was proposing to *do something to* our son that felt threatening and violent to me. The irony is that I have spent years of my professional life sitting across the table from other school administrators, acting as an ally to and advocate for other families while they asked the powers that be across those tables to please include their child, and I have vociferously defended the right of other people's children *to be included.*

As noted by Baglieri et al. (2011), embedded within these advocacy efforts was recognition of the taken-for-granted assumption "that the 'natural' position of this group is one of dis-belonging" (p. 2123). Following a personal history of experiencing individualized, specialized, and often segregated early intervention and preschool experiences, the family of a disabled child is put in the unenviable position of having to actively ask for, claim, assert, and defend their child's right to a seat in a classroom at their neighborhood school. My son, in contrast, already had such a seat (an artifact of the ableist privilege that he experienced upon entering school), and that seat, and its invisible ableist privilege were now in jeopardy. The threat on the table before us was that he could lose that seat if and when they "included" him in the fourth grade designated "inclusion" classroom (which was, of course the classroom where the fourth graders with IEPs were relegated en masse). We had initiated the meeting with the principal to ask that he be transferred to another teacher's classroom. There was one teacher in the fourth grade who was known as a constructivist teacher, and who did inquiry-based curriculum units with her students. While Nicky's teacher was a skilled and competent and thoughtful teacher, she was very directive and skills-oriented not at all constructivist in her pedagogical approach, and after an incredibly difficult year the previous year, we knew after only a couple of weeks that this approach to pedagogy would not be a good fit for his needs at that time.

7 In Search of Meaning, Relevance and Responsiveness, Not *"Pieces of Things"*

Nicky needed, above all else, *meaning* and *relevance* and *responsiveness* in his schooling. During the third grade, within the span of five weeks, he had

SEEKING THE REAL IN AN UNREAL WORLD

experienced a succession of traumatizing personal events that included the death of a beloved grandparent, the death of the one and only teacher that he had ever cherished, the witnessing of a frightening near-death medical emergency of another grandparent, and finally his own hospitalization for a medically necessary surgery, including a traumatizing episode of medical restraint, which he experienced and responded to as to a rape. Returning to school following these events he seemed to be experiencing a prolonged state of both shock and grief, to say nothing of post-traumatic stress, and he simply could not bring himself to care about test prep during the school day and hours of meaningless worksheet completion for homework every evening. We were hoping that a switch to the classroom of the constructivist teacher may provide an opportunity for him to have something to care about in his schooling, for there to be something that interested him enough to make it worthwhile to engage fully again. Perhaps an interdisciplinary unit on rainforests in this teacher's classroom might capture his attention and his willingness to engage with the world more than a basal textbook was proving it could. Consistent with Heshusius' experiences as a public school special educator, Nicky was experiencing school as "pieces of things—pieces without any context, without any meaning. Unreal." And, just as Heshusius reported, "this piecemeal approach to teaching and learning literally drove [him] just about out of [his] mind" (Heshusius, 1996a, p. 53).

Our request was unilaterally denied by the principal, despite the fact that his current classroom teacher also thought it would be a good decision for Nicky's education. We were told that if we were looking for *relevance* in his education, the single most *relevant* factor to him (the principal) was the fact that his standardized test scores had dropped 50 percentile points from the previous year (due to the fact that he simply didn't complete half of the test this year, but instead sat weeping under his desk and turned it in blank). According to the principal, this meant that he was now "a remedial student." Only students with high test scores are placed in the room with the constructivist teacher, we were told, and his current scores didn't indicate that he "could handle it." We were told that there was one, and only one, "ticket out of his current classroom": His choices were to shape up and get his test scores back up where they should be (and stay in his current classroom), or, we could consent to having him evaluated by the district's school psychologist, and then, "*We can include him*," which would be his ticket out.

In that moment I felt (like a punch to the gut) the ontological violence that my son had been testifying to for all those years—they do tell too many lies in there. By saying "We can include him," what I actually heard in that moment was "We can exclude him." Let's consider his assertion that there was only one "ticket out" of his fourth-grade classroom—one that involved eligibility evaluation (which, we noted, it was presumed would result in positive "identification" of disability) and subsequently "including him" (in a classroom that, we also noted, would be even more mind-numbingly drill-oriented than the one we were trying to get him out of). The principal's offer to "include him" was almost certainly not intended as a malevolent threat (although we experienced it as such). But his ontological claim was false: Our only choices were not misery and failure or submitting to disablement and subsequent exclusion (sorry—"inclusion"). In that moment, my husband and I looked at each other and knew with utter certainty that there was in fact another "ticket out" for our son—one that we had already discussed, albeit somewhat reluctantly. I so value the concept of public education that I had been willing to continue to subject my own son to it long after it ceased to be beneficial to him and well into its actively harming him. But this conversation proved to be the tipping point. We would no longer be forced to pretend that the unreal life was real. We informed the principal at that moment that there was actually a second ticket out of his classroom—we were going to withdraw him from public school and homeschool him. To say that the principal was not supportive of this decision would be a monumental understatement (but that is another story). So we made our arrangements, took our son home at the end of that week, and have never looked back. He has been learning at home for almost five years now.

8 What Lives "Beyond"?: Moving beyond the Dividedness Within

After inviting Nicky's testimony about how he had experienced schooling with his body, I then asked him how his body felt now that he was no longer in school:

> In homeschool, I feel like I'm the king of the world. It was the first time I had actually learned something ever in school. My brain seemed to start working again. Real learning has nothing to do with regular school. I felt for the first time in about a year, I actually broke my record of being happy for one solid day. At homeschool, my feelings feel part of me again. Now that I'm in homeschool, I'm really me all of the time, and I have been since the last day of September of 2011.

Homeschooling has not been the complete panacea for his fragmentation that he here describes it as, but I can say that it has enabled us to step back from the brink of the abyss we were teetering over—dissociation, destructive

SEEKING THE REAL IN AN UNREAL WORLD

externalization, and trading his "real existence for a delusion." He is whole again.

Is my son disabled? I will not address that question, because I do not find the premises of it (that there as such things as "disabled" people and "nondisabled" people, that such identities are static and that they can be meaningfully distinguished) to be legitimate or real, and the asking of it tells me more about the questioner than the answer possibly could about my son. However, what is crystal clear to me is that *his schooling actively disabled him*. My son was nearly destroyed by the cumulative assaults of five long years of being schooled every day, precisely because he perceived and experienced them to be the acts of violence against his own lived ontology that they were and are. They forced him to disassociate what he knew to be real from the mystifying ontological assertions he was surrounded by, to be a robot, to not be himself, to virtually (and almost literally) *not be*.

In many ways, I envy my son his utter certainty in the ontological legitimacy of his own experience, but I would also give anything to relieve him of the painful experience of profound alienation that certainty—juxtaposed with "education" practiced in the service of domination and oppression— has caused him. And us. Heshusius (1996b), in her discussion "on tending the divided self," reflects:

> Using Susan Griffin's (1984, p. 175) words, then, we learn, very young, to disown a part of our own being and trade our real existence for a delusion: "We grow used to ignoring the evidence of our own experience, what we hear or see, what we feel in our own bodies." This dissociation within externalizes into many destructive ways. Awareness of this dividedness within will need to be the never ending starting point for its healing. (p. 135)

Developing this chapter has created for me an opportunity to learn from Heshusius' wisdom in a new context as she now helps me to think about ways of tending, daily, to the remnants of my son's divided self. However, healing this division has raised more questions than it has yielded answers. I no longer experience this division within—simply in relation to my son and his education. I have become and I remain divided within as to the central notions of education and of inclusivity generally. It is no longer a matter of perceiving and of valuing alternative ways of knowing. My dividedness within is now ontological.

Heshusius wrote of her attempts to live within these epistemological and ontological conflicts within educational research, to live within this awareness of the duality of her experience; at the same time, she and Ballard titled their (1996) text *From Positivism to Interpretivism and Beyond*. It is the "beyond," not the interpretivism, that now intrigues me and occupies my sleepless nights. I no longer choose to live within the conflict, within the dissonance, within the disassociation and the divided self. I still long to experience Heshusius' optimism, her joy, but I do not seek it by living *within* the contradictions forged by positivist and neoliberal capitalist conceptualizations of education. I seek it in what lies outside, beyond, in the not-yet-materialized, and I do so while abandoning many of my most foundational concepts and ideas—that education is a universal good, that integration in an oppressive system will yield liberation or belonging, that I know what I thought I knew.

Upon sharing an early draft of this paper with Lous, I remarked that:

> I am still searching, daily, for ontological holism in my life, and for support and guidance, I look to the wisdom and the courage of my mentors. Among these are my son Nicky and Lous Heshusius. I only wish that I might have given him the gift of experiencing Lous as his teacher. She continues to be mine.

Her response to this was simultaneously intensely gratifying and deeply saddening, as she asked me to give Nicky a message, from her. She asked me to please tell him these three things: "That he is a very perceptive boy. That he is a very courageous boy. And that he is right." Her message brought tears to my eyes—I had so hoped that she might say that he was wrong. I had hoped to somehow tap in to her inner spring of hope, of optimism, and possibly even of joy. And although joy remains elusive, I will settle, with gratitude, for solidarity.

References

Aronowitz, S. (2008). *Against schooling: For an education that matters*. Boulder, CO: Paradigm Publishers.

Baglieri, S., Bejoian, L. M., Broderick, A. A., Connor, D. J., & Valle, J. W. (2011). [Re]claiming "inclusive education" toward cohesion in educational reform: Disability studies unravels the myth of the normal child. *Teachers College Record, 113*(10), 2122–2154.

Campbell, F. (2009). *Contours of ableism: The production of disability and abledness*. New York, NY: Palgrave MacMillan.

Charlton, J. (1998). The dimensions of disability oppression: An overview. In J. Charlton (Eds.), *Nothing about us without us: Disability oppression and empowerment* (pp. 21–36). Berkeley, CA: University of California Press.

Davis, L. (2002). *Bending over backwards: Disability, dismodernism, & other difficult positions.* New York, NY: New York University Press.

Graham, L., & Slee, R. (2008). An illusory interiority: Interrogating the discourse/s of inclusion. *Educational Philosophy and Theory, 40*(2), 277–293.

Griffin, S. (1984). Split culture. In S. Kauman (Ed.), *The Schmacher series* (Vol. II). London: Blond & Briggs.

Heshusius, L. (1996a). Of life, real and unreal. In *From positivism to interpretivism and beyond: Tales of transformation in educational & social research [The mind-body connection]* (pp. 50–55). New York, NY: Teachers College Press.

Heshusius, L. (1996b). On tending broken dreams. In *From positivism to interpretivism and beyond: Tales of transformation in educational & social research [The mind-body connection]* (pp. 128–135). New York, NY: Teachers College Press.

Heshusius, L., & Ballard, K. (Eds.). (1996). *From positivism to interpretivism and beyond: Tales of transformation in educational & social research [The mind-body connection].* New York, NY: Teachers College Press.

Holt, J. (1976/2004). *Instead of education: Ways to help people do things better.* Boulder, CO: Sentient Publications.

Illich, I. (1970). *Deschooling society.* London: Marion Boyers.

Taylor, S. (1988). Caught in the continuum: A critical analysis of the mandate of the least restrictive environment. *The Journal of the Association for Persons with Severe Handicaps, 13*(1), 41–53.

Valente, J. M. (2011). *d/Deaf and d/Dumb: A portrait of a deaf kid as a young superhero.* New York, NY: Peter Lang.

CHAPTER 4

Reflexivity with and without Self: Lous Heshusius' Purposeless Listening Exercise

Julie Allan

Abstract

This chapter captures the actual rendering of an intervention with preservice teachers who are called upon by Allan to explore their ideological positioning utilizing "participatory consciousness" as outlined by Heshusius. In brief, the call to interrogate unconscious biases about children, disability, and teaching, these undergraduate students found the intervention challenging and welcoming. The key component, as described by Heshusius, was for educators to listen to the call to control and limit lives that often results from unreflective practice.

Keywords

teacher preparation – power practices – reflective practice – bias – disability studies

1   Introduction

> When he grew old, Aristotle, who is not generally considered exactly a tightrope walker, liked to lose himself in the most labrynthine and subtle of discourses. He had then arrived at the age of mētis: "The more solitary and isolated I became, the more I come to like stories." (de Certeau, 1984, p. 90)

Learning to teach fundamentally involves learning from others, whether through their stories or from their perspectives, and which may be filtered or mediated. However, as Heshusius (1995) argues, attention to others that is shaped by one's own concerns impairs one's capacity to 'really listen' (p. 117). Such an inability—or unwillingness—to listen is, according to Nicholas

© KONINKLIJKE BRILL NV, LEIDEN, 2020 | DOI: 10.1163/9789004427280_005

REFLEXIVITY WITH AND WITHOUT SELF

Kristof, an endemic feature of our own society, exhibited through a phenomenon he calls the 'daily me'.

> There's pretty good evidence that we generally don't truly want good information—but rather information that confirms our prejudices. We may believe intellectually in the clash of opinions, but in practice we like to embed ourselves in the reassuring womb of an echo chamber. (Kristof, 2009)

Furthermore, we are inclined not to use rational arguments to influence others, but to appeal to the age-old technique of motive:

> Here is another trick, which, as soon as it is practicable, makes all others unnecessary. Instead of working on your opponent's intellect by argument, work on his will by motive, and he, and also the audience if they have similar interests, will at once be won over by your opinion, even though you got it out of a lunatic asylum. (Schopenhauer, 1896, p. xxxv)

Heshusius (1992) also notes a propensity to dismiss those views that are epistemologically different from ours as 'ideological' or 'dogmatic' (p. 472) whilst never acknowledging our own as such. It is particularly troubling if student teachers, placed formally in a listening and learning role, struggle to listen. Furthermore, if they are unable to listen effectively to their students' voices, including those voices that are diverse, they may contribute actively to the deepening of inequalities.

Heshusius' (1995) exercise in purposeless listening is an important way for beginning teachers to discover the obfuscating effects of their concerns with self and to practise letting go of these concerns to achieve a high level of attentiveness to the Other. This paper reports on the experiences of undergraduate students who were asked to take part in a conversation with a young person and to reflect upon the nature of self and the relationship with the Other within that conversation. The conversation took place within a context in which the student teachers were evaluating the usefulness of the medical and social models of disability in enabling them to understand the difficulties of children they had recently taught. The paper reports how student teachers' efforts to let go of the self, through the purposeless listening exercise, led to a more sophisticated understanding of the role and function of reflexivity, their capacity to attend to others, and their ability to engage with different models of understanding disability. It also provoked in the students, a recognition of the possibility that they might 'listen less' to some of the more unhelpful guidance from experienced teachers. The students' recognition of the need to be more discerning about listening to experienced teachers, whilst at the same time needing to be seen to be appreciative and responsive is understood, following Derrida (1992, 1993) as an aporetic demand. This consists of double contradictory imperatives neither of which can ever be wholly satisfied, but which both have to be responded to. The students' way of managing the aporia within their placement school is interpreted, following C. Wright Mills (2000), as practising an identity as a 'Wobbly'. The paper begins with an account of the particular demands for reflexivity faced by student teachers. It then reports on the listening exercise that was set for the students, the results from this and the students' accounts of what they heard when they 'really' listened to children. The paper then explores student teachers' accounts of the experienced teachers to whom they were constrained to listen and what they heard of teachers' understanding of disability and difference. It also examines how the student teachers, whilst trying to get to grips with the social model of disability, heard teachers' almost exclusive use of medicalised and deficit models when speaking of particular children. It concludes with an outline of a framework, developed from and with the student teachers, for both listening more (and better) to children and listening less to experienced teachers in schools.

2   Becoming Teacher, Becoming Reflexive

Teacher education, as it is currently configured, does little to promote reflexivity among beginning teachers. They are expected to develop a high level of reflexivity, as part of their set of competences, but this often stops short of reflection in practice (Allan & Slee, 2008). Even if they succeed in articulating multiple selves (Peshkin, 1988), discerning the way in which these selves interact with their practice and accommodate competing 'spaces of points of view' (Bourdieu, 1999), this hyper-vigilance of self and others can lead to a form of 'vanity reflexivity' (Kenway & McLeod, 2004, p. 528) or narcissism (Krizek, 2003). Heshusius (1995) suggests that the 'self-as-teacher identity' (p. 122) that student teachers are made to cultivate encourages them to see themselves as having nothing in common with the young people they teach.

Such a failure to prepare student teachers to have regard for others is not surprising when we consider the extent to which teacher education is currently 'under siege' (Sleeter, 2008, p. 1947) from neoliberalist policies. As Sleeter points out, curricula have become increasingly prescribed, controlled and scripted, together with the expectation that teachers will deliver this faithfully and teacher education has degenerated into a form of technical support geared towards raising student test scores. The removal of educational studies and the general reduction of theoretical content from courses has been acknowledged by many as a global phenomenon (Sleeter, 2008; Furlong & Lawn, 2009; Beach & Bagley, 2012) but Dennis Beach (2012) draws on Basil Bernstein to highlight the negative impact this has had on beginning teachers' thinking. Bernstein (1999) distinguishes between a horizontal, the everyday, discourse, linked to commonsense understandings and often tacit, oral and context specific, and a vertical discourse, produced within Universities and which offers 'a scientific 'know why' discourse'. The erosion of the vertical discourse (through a move away from an emphasis on scientific praxis or the removal of philosophy of education) could, Bernstein suggests, be part of a move to undermine the knowledge interests of a professional discourse and open them up to influences. But as others have argued (Apple, 2001; Beach, 2012; Sleeter, 2008; Lauder, Brown, & Halsey, 2009; Oancea & Bridges, 2009), the erosion of the vertical discourse removes the capacity of beginning teachers to think critically and to understand the global influences on their profession and of their selves precisely at a time when the effects are considerable. Furthermore, the absence of this discourse, and the criticality that comes with it, may leave teachers less able to recognize the competing demands of equity and choice and therefore find a balance between them (Alexandersson, 2011) and make them in turn at greater risk of political manipulation and economic exploitation (Sleeter, 2008).

The textbooks on teaching—'the big glossies' (Brantlinger, 2006, p. 67)—emphasise the teacher self and its distance from children. They emphasise the need to 'plan, manage, direct, assess—in other words to have an array of predetermined purposes for interacting with youngsters' (Heshusius, 1995, p. 122)—and increase the distance from them further. Furthermore, the textbooks pathologise and typologise children's difficulties and project a level of confidence and certainty that they can be managed effectively in the classroom (Allan, 2008). They affect to help students to 'know' students with particular kinds of pathologies by presenting them a segmented way, without regard for the intersections of disability with class, race, gender, sexuality or any other aspect of diversity. Their purpose is purely in skilling beginning teachers at hunting down difference (Graham, 2014). The realities presented in these texts bear little resemblance to the children whom the student teachers encounter, add to their confusion and anxiety about how to respond to individuals and ensure that sight is lost of 'what matters' (Ferri, Gallagher, & Connor, 2011, p. 222). They also place teachers and 'difficult' students in opposition to each other (Slee, 2011) and construct teaching as being about control and management of students by teachers. Consequently, notes Slee (2011, p. 86), 'teachers often feel at a loss and are personally distressed about the difficulties experienced by disabled children in their classrooms'. Their anxieties are particularly acute where children with behavioural problems are concerned (Harwood & Allan, 2014).

The proliferation of disability narratives, aimed ostensibly at offering insights into the world of disabled people, achieves little in this regard. Hacking (2010, p. 632) notes a particular growth, indeed a 'boom industry,' in autism narrative, with fiction and non-fiction as well as other media forms specifically about individuals diagnosed as autistic. This genre promotes, through 'terrible psychology' (ibid., p. 654), understandings of autistic individuals as having special attributes neurotypicals lack and tells us, according to Hacking, less about autism itself but more about the times in which we live. This storytelling orientation also appears to feed the thirst, among the public and professionals, for *knowing* the autistic person and reinforces the 'morbid fascination for the odd' (Hacking, 2010, p. 641). It seems unlikely to make beginning teachers any more capable of listening to disabled children.

Heshusius, whose own reflexivity was honed and elaborated in two remarkable books recounting her experience of living with chronic pain, describes the challenge of letting go of the self in order to engage in the present (2009, 2017). In Heshusius' case, this involved letting go of the intense desire to be cured but ultimately allowed her to 'maintain some sense of sanity and coherence in the face of constant pain' and 'brought moments of peace and beauty' (Heshusius, Fishman, & Morris, 2009, p. 14) and the kind of 'brilliant imperfection' that Eli Claire (2016) also realised.

3 The Listening Exercise

Thirteen undergraduate student teachers, in their third year of study of a concurrent teacher education programme (in which they studied professional education alongside their undergraduate study of subjects taught at high school, such as maths, English and history), were asked to undertake 'a "purposeless" assignment' (Heshusius, 1995, p. 117), involving a conversation with a young person. Following Heshusius' approach, students were asked 'to just be with a youngster and listen' (p. 118). Unlike Heshusius, however, it was not stipulated that the student should not know the young person, so the students could choose someone with whom they were familiar. Students were advised that the objective of the conversation was to listen and that they should, above all, avoid conducting the conversation as an interview, with them asking all the

REFLEXIVITY WITH AND WITHOUT SELF

questions and retaining control. They were asked to make notes and to discuss at a subsequent seminar, again following Heshusius:

1. How the conversation went—what was said and in what way
2. The students' personal reactions to the conversation—what it illuminated for them; What they felt thought, looked forward to, worried about, enjoyed, didn't enjoy, before, during and after the conversation and why.

The students returned with copious notes and with much to say about their encounter with the young person they had met; they also made connections with the types of listening that they were expected to undertake as student teachers, some of which they had found unhelpful. The student teachers reported finding the assignment challenging and difficult and, like Heshusius' (1995) student teachers, saw its purposeless as unusual, but not negatively so. However they described their anxiety about undertaking this task, which the student teachers had also reported to Heshusius. Their fears were less related to having nothing in common, as Heshusius had found, but were more concerned with being taken seriously by the young people as wanting to listen and with worries about 'saying something stupid'.

3.1 *How Hard It Is to (Really) Listen*

Several students commented on how difficult they found listening attentively to children, realising, through the exercise, how much they tended to dominate conversations, control them through questioning or interrupt:

> I found myself wanting to keep asking questions when the conversation would trail off a bit. However I knew I should be trying not to lead so I tried really hard to simply add to the subject rather than asking the questions.
>
> I found out how hard it is to listen. I realise I keep interrupting. I had to force myself not to speak and that was hard.

One student teacher described the challenge for her being not the listening itself, but being careful to avoid being judgemental in ways that could be discerned by the child, for example through gesture or posture. This individual was also concerned about the possibility of the child disclosing something to her that she would need to pass on out of a regard for child protection.

One student teacher described being unable to establish a conversation with a youngster and concluded that he 'simply couldn't speak and was socially awkward'. Her judgement was of the young person rather than of herself and she had evidently failed to grasp the exercise. Another student reported finding listening to a young person relatively easy but it became clear that she had directed the conversation with a series of questions.

3.2   *Boundary Work*

A few of the student teachers felt that they had been successful in, as Heshusius suggests, blurring the boundaries between adult and child.

> I felt slightly awkward myself in generating a conversation with a young child from nowhere, and I thought that they would find it difficult to talk openly and comfortably with me. As the conversation progressed, I started to feel relaxed, at ease and happy as we were comfortable enough talking with each other—almost as equals, rather than 'adult and child'. I was worried that the child was going to get a little 'too' comfortable within the conversation and start acting as though they were talking with one of their peers: however, this was not the case and the child kept the conversation flowing whilst being very respectful.

A student teacher who was concerned about the child disclosing confidential information during the conversation indicated that this concern had arisen because of her sense that the child was perceiving her as not quite an adult. This, she felt, would make children more likely to open up and disclose to her than they would to the other 'proper adults'.

3.3   *Achieving Participatory Consciousness*

A small number of student teachers succeeded in reaching a state that Heshusius (1995) refers to as participatory consciousness and they described this as a relaxed state of hyper-attentiveness in which the conversation 'flowed':

> The conversation was slow to start but once I had established some common ground, i.e., a like of lego, then it flowed more easily ... The conversation was very enthusiastic.

Like Heshusius, the students felt both quiet and alive while they were listening. The warmth of the exchange was also a significant aspect of the successful conversations for the students and while Heshusius described the achievement of a forgetfulness of her own self, these students seemed to still be focusing on themselves. They were, however, attuned to parts of themselves and their identities that surprised and pleased them:

> The conversation highlighted my warm, caring nature towards children and reinforced to me that my rapport with children is one of my strengths.
>
> It was easy to listen and I felt that I was being a good listener. An autistic boy I work with told me about the new washing machine his mum had got. He told me about how it worked and felt such great pleasure at being chosen to hear his story.

Heshusius may consider these students to have failed to let go of themselves; alternatively they may have reached a transition stage where they were attending to themselves as they listened, an experience that Heshusius herself described as informative. For one student teacher, the achievement of participatory consciousness enabled her to both listen and hear what she had been told before but had not taken seriously. Because the student teachers were not restricted to having a conversation with someone they barely knew, one individual decided to talk to her own daughter. During this encounter, the student teacher heard, for the first time, about the extreme difficulties that her daughter was experiencing at school, which included bullying. When she had listened to her daughter telling her this previously, she had put it down to the usual troubles between teenage girls; when she began to *really* listen, she came to understand the nature and extent of the difficulties and felt a sense of shame. She was, however, able to put things right for her daughter.

Another student teacher revealed her own already established practice for achieving what she came to understand through the listening exercise as participatory consciousness. She operated what she called a 'moaning seat' (moaning being a colloquial term for getting things off one's chest), which was either the front passenger seat of her car or the seat beside her computer at home. In each case, eye contact with the talker was not possible and the student teacher's attention to another task—driving or typing—enabled her to achieve the kind of relaxed concentration which was necessary in order to listen.

The student teachers declared their satisfaction with the listening assignment because of the way in which it had alerted them to the challenge of *really* listening and to the need to work at this, and on themselves, in their teaching. This also provoked for them a critical attention to the listening they were expected, and possibly required, to do within their placement schools. The experienced teachers to whom they were constrained to listen often said things that were at best unhelpful and at worst were profoundly negative and this was particularly apparent in relation to disabled students. Student teachers reported having to listen to, and observe, what amounted to strategies of (in)difference towards individual pupils and teacher talk about disabled students which was itself disabling.

4 Strategies of (In)Difference

The student teachers described how troubled they were by the way in which the mentors in their placement schools discussed disability and difference with them. These experienced individuals were advising the student teachers on how to assess, teach and support disabled children and were also evaluating their teaching performance. The student teachers felt an obligation to be seen to be responsive to advice and support from the teachers, yet struggled to find much of this helpful and often found it deeply unsettling. They identified four strategies of (in)difference to students and their special educational needs:

4.1 Dismissal of Individual Students
Student teachers revealed their discomfort with how teachers often described individual children with negative reference to their behaviour or in ways which pronounced their failure: 'he just can't learn'. Some children were described in relation to difficult home circumstances with a clear implication that these, and their parents, were the major causes of their failure. The student teachers reported feeling dismayed by the sense of futility surrounding these young people.

4.2 Collective Othering
The student teachers were attentive to the power of language to both separate out individual children and to ascribe a collective identity to them. Students with special educational needs or students with a particular diagnosis such as ADHD were heard being referred to as 'all of them'; 'they,' or by the label itself, with teachers, for example speaking of having 'three ADHDs' in her class. The detailed information that the student teachers were seeking about individual children was often obscured by this collective othering and rendering of them as 'extravisible' (Goode, 2007, p. 41), but only in a general sense.

4.3 The 'Need to Know'
A concern for confidentiality led some schools to withhold information from teachers and student teachers. In other cases, information came more informally and via the teachers themselves. Student teachers felt uncertain about what they could expect to find out about children and about factors, such as home circumstances, that could have a bearing on their learning. In one case a student teacher told of her distress in hearing teachers engaging in the

REFLEXIVITY WITH AND WITHOUT SELF

dismissal of one individual child who appeared to make no effort in class. The student teacher subsequently learned that the child had been exhausted in class because of extremely difficult home circumstances.

4.4 Guess the Deficit

The most bizarre strategy reported involved the teacher making the student teacher guess which children belonged to particular special needs labels. The student teacher, in spite of being discomfited by such an expectation, felt the need to play along and, to her mentor's satisfaction, was able to guess the deficits, and the associated children, correctly.

5 Talking about Disability in School

The social model of disability was developed by disabled scholars and activists, most notably Vic Finkelstein (1980) and Mike Oliver (1996), as an alternative to the medicalising or deficit oriented understanding of disability. It shifted the locus of the problem as being within the individual to being situated in the practices of institutions and societies and, according to the social model, disability is produced through the interaction of an individual's impairment with barriers which may be environmental, structural or attitudinal. The social model of disability also marks a shift, in C. Wright Mills' (1959) terms, from disability being a private trouble to it being a public issue. Whilst the social model represents an enlightened view of disablement, and one which teachers can do something about by seeking to remove disabling barriers, one of its founding forefathers, Mike Oliver, laments the fact that it has never been properly *used*:

> I wish people would stop talking about it. The social model is not some kind of conceptual device to debate. The social model is a tool that we should use to try and produce changes in the world, changes in what we do. What I hoped from that was that people would start using it and then what we would actually see was not 'what are the theoretical underpinnings of the social model? Mike Oliver says this and Jenny Morris says that and somebody else says that.' You know, complete rehashes of that, but 'this is what I did with the social model. This is how I took it into a particular school or particular social work agency. This is what we did with it and this is whether it worked or not. (Allan & Slee, 2008, p. 88)

Oliver's frustration that the social model has remained at the level of debate and reflection led to him retiring as an academic, filled with 'pain and disillusionment' (1999, p. 185). In a subsequent head-to-head between Mike Oliver and Tom Shakespeare, the utility of the social model was brought into question with Shakespeare (2006, p. 9) arguing that disability studies, especially in the UK, was in an 'impasse' and that what has caused it to become 'stagnated' (p. 1), the social model, should be abandoned:

> Disability studies would be better off without the social model, which has become fatally undermined by its own contradictions and inadequacies. To reject the British social model does not mean returning to the bad old days of medicalisation and individualistic approaches before the UPIAS revolution. There are many other, more robust, ways of conceptualising disability, which retain a commitment to equality and justice for disabled people, but do not base the analysis on a mistaken bracketing of disability difference. (Shakespeare, 2006, p. 28)

Oliver responded by denouncing this view and the book in which it featured as 'a mish mash of contradictory perspectives' (Oliver, 2007, p. 230).

The student teachers reported an overwhelming focus by teachers in their placement schools on medicalised understandings of children's special educational needs. They found little or no acknowledgement of disablement arising from environmental, structural or attitudinal barriers within the school. The medicalisation of children's behaviour, using diagnoses of Attention Deficit Hyperactivity Disorder (ADHD), was particularly striking for the student teachers who returned from their placement with a sense of, if not an epidemic, at least a significant concentration of students apparently 'suffering' from this disorder. Most unsettling for them was their accompanying sense of uncertainty about what, precisely, ADHD is and this is hardly surprising given its contested nature and the suspicions about motives behind increasing rates of diagnosis (Harwood, 2010). For one student in particular, the teacher's acceptance of a dyspraxia diagnosis meant that they had identified various activities that he would be unable to manage; the student teacher thought that a more nuanced understanding of how the child's learning would be affected by dyspraxia would have been more appropriate, but this was not forthcoming.

6 Listening More *and* Less

The student teachers concluded this assignment with an assertion of their desire—and intention—to listen more, and more intensively, to children and to listen less, whilst appearing to do so, to the experienced teachers within their placement schools. They recognised their own (teacherly) selves as getting in the way of being attentive to the children and the listening exercise had demonstrated to them how the 'noise' that they generated themselves intruded on their listening. They understood Heshusius' (1995) enjoinder that 'To hear youngsters we must get ourselves out of the way' (p. 122). The student teachers appeared intent on turning down that noise in order to listen more effectively. When it came to the experienced teachers in their placement school the student teachers expressed a desire to listen less to what they were being told, especially about disability and difference, such was the damaging and negative nature of it. However, they also recognised that they had an obligation to be seen to taking up the advice and guidance of those teachers who ultimately had a say in the assessment of their placement. Derrida (1992) refers to this double contradictory imperative or two competing obligations as an 'aporia' (p. 22) which creates a problem of 'not knowing where to go' (Derrida, 1993, p. 12). Derrida suggests that an aporia is a necessary ordeal of impossibility which one has to go through in order to make a decision and take responsibility and it is only when one acknowledges an aporia that justice is possible:

> The paralysis that it connotes, the aporia for me, is not paralysis, it is a chance; it is a chance; not so-called 'luck,' but something which conditions affirmation, decision and responsibility. (p. 63)

The student teachers appeared to manage this aporetic demand by practising an identity whilst on placement which C. Wright Mills (2000) calls a 'Wobbly'.

> I am a Wobbly. I mean this spiritually and politically. In saying this I refer less to political orientation that to political ethos, and I take Wobbly to mean one thing: the opposite of bureaucrat. [...] I am a Wobbly, personally, down deep, and for good. I am outside the whale, and I got that way through social isolation and self-help. But do you know what a Wobbly is? It's a kind of spiritual condition. Don't be afraid of the word, Tovarich. A Wobbly is not only a man who takes orders from himself. He's also a man who's often in the situation where there are no regulations to fall back upon that he hasn't made up himself. He doesn't like bosses—capitalistic or communistic—they are all the same to him. He wants to be, and he wants everyone else to be, his own boss at all times under all conditions and for any purposes they may want to follow up. This kind of spiritual condition, and only this, is Wobbly freedom. (p. 252)

Although Mills' notion of a Wobbly was connected with the political dissidents of the first world war, the quiet resistance and will to develop new systems, whilst avoiding any particular allegiance, it seems an apt way of depicting how the students' positioned themselves in their placement school.

7   Concluding Thoughts

Heshusius (2004) alerts us to the exclusionary nature of 'separative' practices (p. 147), through which we seek to maintain a distance from the Other and, in so doing, allow our own ego to dominate and obscure what the Other has to say. The listening exercise, constructed by Heshusius (2005) and undertaken by my own student teachers, enabled them to realise the troubling nature of their own selves and the possibility that they—and their ego—could impede inclusion. This is significant and denotes a very particular form of reflexivity that is both critical, in bringing aspects of their selves to attention, and productive, in alerting them to ways in which they can let go, even if just for a short while.

The listening exercise appeared to make the student teachers more inclined to listen to what was being said within their placement schools about the children. Although the student teachers were troubled by what they heard, they had possibly begun to acquire skills in a kind of reflexivity that had at its heart a concern with power relations. This recognised the students' vulnerable position but also allowed them to affect to listen and receive wisdom gratefully whilst actually attending to it only selectively. Some of what they chose to edit out of the teachers' stories was the strongly medicalised view of disability and difference and the negative and pathologising strategies that often accompanied these.

The listening exercise, through the practice it gives in attending to other than the self, has the potential to cultivate among student teachers what Spivak (1993, p. 63) considers a necessary kind of 'vigilence' to render them alert to inequalities:

> For the long haul emancipatory social intervention is not primarily a question of redressing victimage by the assertion of (class- or gender- or ethnocultural identity. It is a question of developing a vigilence for systematic appropriations of the unacknowledged social production of a *differential* that is one basis of exchange into the networks of the cultural politics of class- or gender-*identification*. (original emphasis)

REFLEXIVITY WITH AND WITHOUT SELF

It also has the potential to enable student teachers to acquire a knowledge about the Other that is not dependent on their similarity to the Other, nor on their capacity to 'identify' with the Other. Rather, their knowledge can be sustained, as Spivak (1987 p. 254) reminds us by 'irreducible difference'. Thus, student teachers' can approach the task of coming to know the children in their class as a 'continued struggle with the self' (Heshusius, 2004, p153). This, according to Ware (2004, p. 184) is a 'hopeful' orientation, driven by a sense that it might be possible to know children better, and an obligation towards children that comes from a heightened sense of the risk to them of exclusion. As Foucault (1984) reminds us, recognising danger means 'we always have something to do' and leads us 'not to apathy but to a hyper- and pessimistic activism' (p. 343).

References

Alexandersson, M. (2011). Equivalence and choice in combination: The Swedish dilemma. *Oxford Review of Education, 37*, 195–214.

Allan, J. (2008). *Rethinking inclusive education: The philosophers of difference in practice.* Dordrecht: Springer.

Allan, J., & Slee, R. (2008). *Doing inclusive education research.* Rotterdam, The Netherlands: Sense Publishers.

Apple, M. W. (2001). Markets, standards, teaching, and teacher education. *Journal of Teacher Education, 52*(3), 182–196.

Beach, D. (2012, April 26–27). *Sixty years of policy development in teacher education in Sweden: Changing professional discourses in teacher education policy.* Keynote address at the International Conference on the Transformation of School and Teacher Professionalism, Gothenburg.

Beach, D., & Bagley, C. (2012). The weakening role of education studies and the re-traditionalisation of Swedish teacher education. *Oxford Review of Education, 38*(3), 287–303.

Bernstein, B. (1999). Vertical and horizontal discourse: An essay. *British Journal of Sociology of Education, 20*(2), 157–173.

Bourdieu, P. (1999). *The weight of the world.* London: Sage.

Brantlinger, E. (2006). The big glossies: How textbooks structure (special) education. In E. Brantlinger (Ed.), *Who benefits from special education? Remediating (fixing) other people's children.* Mahwah, NJ: Lawrence Erlbaum Associates.

Claire, E. (2016). *Introduction to Brilliant imperfection: Grappling with cure.* Retrieved January 20, 2016, from http://eliclare.com/book-news/writing-a-mosaic

de Certeau, M. (1985). *The practice of everyday life*. Berkeley, CA: University of California Press.

Derrida, J. (1992). Force of law: The mystical foundation of authority (M. Quaintance, Trans.). In D. Cornell, M. Rosenfield, & D. Carlson (Eds.), *Deconstruction and the possibility of justice*. New York, NY: Routledge.

Derrida, J. (1993). *Aporias*. Stanford, CA: Stanford University Press.

Ferri, B., Gallagher, D., & Connor, D. (2011). Pluralizing methodologies in the field of LD: From what works to what matters. *Learning Disability Quarterly, 34*(3), 222–231.

Finkelstein, V. (1980). *Attitudes and disabled people*. New York, NY: World Rehabilitation Fund.

Foucault, M. (1984). On the genealogy of ethics: An overview of work in progress. In P. Rabinow (Ed.), *The Foucault reader*. New York, NY: Pantheon.

Furlong, J., & Lawn, M. (2009). The disciplines of education in the UK: Between the ghost and the shadow. *Oxford Review of Education, 35*(5), 541–552.

Goode, J. (2007). 'Managing' disability: Early experiences of university students with disabilities, *Disability & Society, 22*(1), 35–48.

Graham, L. (2014). A little learning is a dangerous thing. Factors influencing the increased identification of special educational needs from the perspective of education policy-makers and school practitioners. *International Journal of Disability Development and Education*. doi:10.1080/1034912X.2014.955791

Hacking, I. (2010). Autism fiction? A mirror of an internet decade? *University of Toronto Quarterly, 79*, 632–655.

Harwood, V. (2010). The new outsiders: ADHD and disadvantage. In L. J. Graham (Ed.), *(De)constructing ADHD: Critical guidance for teachers and teacher educators*. New York, NY: Peter Lang.

Harwood, V., & Allan, J. (2014). *Psychopathology at school: Theorizing mental disorder in education*. Abingdon: Routledge.

Heshusius, L. (1992). Reading meaning into texts. *Exceptional Children, 58*(5), 472–475.

Heshusius, L. (1995). Listening to children: What could we possibly have in common? From concerns with self to participatory consciousness. *Theory into Practice, 34*(2), 117–123.

Heshusius, L. (2004). Special education knowledges: The inevitable struggle with the 'self'. In L. Ware (Ed.), *Ideology and the politics of (in)exclusion*. New York, NY: Peter Lang.

Heshusius, L. (2017). *Experiencing chronic pain in society*. Self published. Amazon.com

Heshusius, L., Fishman, S. M., & Morris, D. B. (2009). *Inside chronic pain: An intimate and critical account*. New York, NY: Cornell University Press.

Kenway, J., & McLeod, J. (2004). Bourdieu's reflexive sociology and 'spaces of points of view': Whose reflexivity, which perspective? *British Journal of Sociology of Education, 25*(4), 525–544.

REFLEXIVITY WITH AND WITHOUT SELF

Kristof, N. (2009, March 18). The daily me. *The New York Times*.

Krizek, R. (2003). Ethnography as the excavation of personal narrative. In R. Clair (Ed.), *Expressions of ethnography* (pp. 141–151). Albany, NY: SUNY Press.

Lauder, H., Brown, P., & Halsey, A. H. (2009). Sociology of education: A critical history and prospects for the future. *Oxford Review of Education, 35*(5), 569–585.

Oancea, A., & Bridges, D. (2009). Philosophy of education in the UK: The historical and contemporary tradition. *Oxford Review of Education, 35*(5), 553–568.

Oliver, M. (1996). *Understanding disability: From theory to practice.* Basingstoke: Macmillan Press.

Oliver, M. (1999). Final accounts and the parasite people. In M. Corker & S. French (Eds.), *Disability discourse.* Buckingham: Open University Press.

Oliver, M. (2007). Contribution to review symposium (untitled). *Disability and Society, 22*(2), 230–234.

Peshkin, A. (1988, October). In search of subjectivity—One's own. *Educational Researcher,* 17(7), 17–21.

Schopenhauer, A. (1896). *The art of controversy.* New York, NY: Cosimo.

Shakespeare, T. (2006). *Disability rights and wrongs.* London: Routledge.

Slee, R. (2011). *The irregular school.* London: Routledge.

Sleeter, C. (2008). Equity, democracy, and neo-liberal assaults on teacher education. *Teaching and Teacher Education, 24*(8), 1947–1957.

Spivak, G. C. (1987). *In other worlds: Essays in cultural politics.* New York, NY: Methuen.

Spivak, G. C. (1993). *Outside in the teaching machine.* New York, NY: Routledge.

Ware, L. (2004). The politics of ideology: A pedagogy of critical hope. In L. Ware (Ed.), *Ideology and the politics of (in)exclusion.* New York, NY: Peter Lang.

Wright Mills, C. (1959). *The sociological imagination.* Oxford, UK: Oxford University Press.

Wright Mills, C. (2000). *Letters and autobiographical writings* (K. Mills with P. Mills, Eds.). Berkeley, CA: University of California Press.

CHAPTER 5

The Illusion of Our Separativeness: Exploring Heshusius' Concept of Participary Conciousness in Disability Research and Inclusive Education

Deborah J. Gallagher

Abstract

This chapter encourages reflexive analysis as the default stance for educators who seek honest exploration of that which troubles us and alienates us from deeper understanding of disability, our students and the teaching process. Gallaher draws from "Freeing Ourselves from Objectivity: Managing Subjectivity or Turning Toward a Participatory Mode of Consciousness" (Heshusisus, 1994), offering her own philosophical treatment of the objectivity/subjectivity debates relative to how we come to know what we believe. Gallagher summons educators and those who prepare educators to respond.

Keywords

philosophy – objectivity – subjectivity – reflexivity – teacher education

If you have ever advocated for inclusive education before an audience of skeptics (or those who imagine that they have a stake in maintaining the status quo), then you know that it takes roughly a nanosecond before you are assailed with apprehensive questions that go something like this: What about the disruptive students? How can we accommodate the needs of special education students without shortchanging the others? Won't they feel humiliated when they can't keep up? Most urgently, though, they insist on knowing how to *do* inclusion, and it's clear that to most people's way of thinking doing inclusion centers on using the right methods and techniques. Along with the discussion of these questions, others of a more philosophical nature will soon be broached—How do we know that this or that particular teaching practice works in an inclusive classroom? Is there *solid* research that supports it (*it*, meaning a particular practice or inclusion writ large)?

© EMERALD GROUP PUBLISHING LIMITED, 2015 | DOI: 10.1163/9789004427280_006

The conversation then becomes all about how-to teaching techniques and what counts as *proof* that these techniques *work*. Agreement about these issues is very hard to come by, though. What some find appealing and compelling gets rejected by others, and the dialog has a remarkable tendency to break down. Those who genuinely want to facilitate inclusion as much as those who are hesitant or even opposed wind up feeling ill at ease, vaguely dissatisfied, and ultimately dispirited. Why is that; and, more importantly, how can it be different?

Centering on the work of Lous Heshusius (1994), I discuss the insights she offered about why this breakdown occurs and how different outcomes are distinctly possible. In doing so, I focus on the problem of methods (both research and teaching) as the core of the problem recounted above. I'll begin with some historical back-grounding which I believe provides a helpful context, followed by a discussion of Heshusius, *Freeing Ourselves from Objectivity: Managing Subjectivity or Turning toward a Participatory Mode of Consciousness*. I conclude with an exploration of how her concept of participatory consciousness can inform progress toward inclusive education.

1   Historical Context

Something both subtle and powerful was operating below the surface of the standard inclusion discussion I described above. Here I'm referring to how so often the centrality of methods and techniques acts as a kind of default setting when educators talk in larger groups about, well, almost anything. This talk around methods is understandable enough given the philosophical perspective on the nature of knowledge (epistemology) and the nature of reality (ontology) that has been paramount in our thinking since the time of the ancient Greeks and the origins of Western philosophy. As this line of thought has worked itself out over the centuries, it eventually arrived at what we call science and the scientific method. At the core of this approach is the idea that properly applied methods will allow us to be objective. By being objective, we'll discover things as they really are, and, ultimately, be able in practice to predict the consequences of our interventions/actions and thereby take control the world around us. According to this perspective, the answers to the inclusion questions can be found in researching the psychology of disruptive students, specific teaching interventions/methods, group dynamics within diverse classrooms, and so on and so on. Ultimately, it is assumed, the application of the scientific methods in educational research will ultimately result in a series of teaching methods, practices, and arrangements that will allow us to achieve inclusive classrooms that work.

All of this sounds very good, especially in that the methodical approach appears to have been enormously successful in the physical sciences (where the whole thing originated and was then imported for the study of social life). However, in the area of educational inquiry/practice, even if less so within the social "sciences" in general, this approach has been subject to very strong, and one could even say, devastating, critiques. If for no other reason, these critiques were driven by the obvious condition that the application of scientific method was not achieving the desired results of allowing educators to accurately predict the consequences of their methods/interventions—and it was not that more and more of this kind of research was needed to achieve this kind of prediction.

Drawing on a series of major challenges to conventional philosophy of science (see Bernstein, 1983; Dewey, 1916, 1938; Gadamer, 1975; Hanson, 1958; Kuhn, 1962; Nagel, 1986; Putnam, 1981; Rorty, 1979), a number of educational philosophers understood these challenges and have argued convincingly that it was not a matter of *doing more* because this approach to the study of human social life was inherently flawed and fatally so. In any event, this challenge to the established methodology in the late 1970s and on through the next decades came to be known as the qualitative-quantitative debates. Because the substance of them is well-traveled terrain, I'll need only briefly to outline the contours.

In a nutshell, opponents argued that the methods of the physical sciences (the scientific method and its attendant tools of quantification, reductionism, and objectivism) were entirely ill-suited for the study of people, the social world, and therefore, education (see Bogdan & Biklen, 1982; Eisner & Peshkin, 1990; Heshusius, 1986, 1989; Iano, 1986; Poplin, 1987; Schwandt, 1980, 1990; Skrtic, 1986, 1991; Smith, 1983, 1989). People, after all, are not *things* that can be brought under scientific prediction and control—even if such prediction and control were ethical, much less desirable. Nor can they be objectified or made into so many objects as such. What's more, the contingencies or "randomness" of the social world preclude such aspirations. Most of all, they argued that human beings and their social worlds are fundamentally about the individual and collective meanings we bring to our lives and how we *make sense* of things. So the questions we seek to answer when we study the social world are, inevitably, *interpretations* of these meanings. It simply cannot be otherwise.

Importantly, it was not that scholars as a group were calling for an all-out ban on the use of quantitative methods, despite the flaws and often overlooked detriments these methods produced. Instead, they simply wanted to make clear that this methodological framework had no grounds for asserting claims to superior knowledge based on unwarranted assertions of objectivity. And in

THE ILLUSION OF OUR SEPARATIVENESS   75

that these assertions were unwarranted, quantitative research methods are no better positioned to adjudicate disputes about knowledge claims than qualitative methods. Because both approaches are tools of interpretation, the former possesses no greater authority than the latter in terms of separating facts from opinions, what works versus what we believe works, and so on.

Not unexpectedly, these challenges to the firmly established and institutionally secure methodology resulted in a rather trenchant divide among educational researchers. On the one side were those who advanced qualitative and interpretivist approaches for conducting research, contending that these methods were not only better suited to the study of education, but also that they avoided the pitfalls of scientific reductionism that tended to obscure or distort what goes on in classrooms and the people who inhabit them. These scholars essentially disputed the trump card status of quantitative research methods in resolving disagreements about "what works" in classrooms.

On the other side of the emerging divide were those who adamantly defended the concept of objectivity (Phillips, 1987) and quantitative research methods as a means to separate facts from opinions—i.e., erect something of a firewall between what they saw as objective facts and researchers' subjective interpretations (see Gage, 1978, 1989; Kauffman, 1987). For them, quantitative research methods represented *real* science—or what later came to be called the "gold standard" of educational research (see: Slavin, 2002). When their detractors continued to point out that these methods cannot, in fact, achieve objectivity, many defenders simply insisted otherwise. Others conceded the point, but not entirely. They argued that even if quantitative methods could not achieve complete objectivity then at least they offered some degree of neutrality. It's an appealing argument until we ask questions like—to what degree and how might we know which part of the research results are objective and which ones are not (for an in-depth discussion of this issue, see Gallagher, 2006)?

Many, many such debates were published in the professional literature, but not much transpired in terms of achieving a workable consensus. And, as the conflicts and clashes continued apace, many scholars began to view the situation not only intractable and unproductive (Stanovich, 1990), but also an exhausting distraction from "real" research. For example, Miles and Huberman (1984) echoed the sentiments of many when they declared that it was time to get back to the business at hand and that "the grand debate should be left to those who care most about it" (p. 20). Eventually, both sides tacitly agreed to live and let live. As Smith and Heshusius (1986) pointed out, though, avoiding these conversations constituted a fatefully squandered opportunity, most certainly because evasion has had the unfortunate effect of "transforming qualitative inquiry into a procedural variation of quantitative inquiry" (p. 8).[1] Most of all, the failure to press on through these important philosophical questions has meant that, to this day, our deliberations about inclusive education are derailed by inchoate concerns about research objectivity and procedural neutrality.

On a practical front, however, qualitative and interpretivist research methods did achieve increased acceptance, although these approaches continued to be viewed as less legitimate (the *weaker sister* of the research world, useful for exploratory studies that contributed ultimately to quantitative research, etc.). And perhaps it was that lack of full institutional acceptance that contributed to qualitative research scholars' attempt to emulate quantitative research by adopting parallel criteria (e.g., trustworthiness, believability, confirmability) and methods (e.g., audit trails, peer debriefing, member checking) as substitutes for the procedures for warranting validity and reliability used in quantitative research (see Guba, 1981; Lincoln & Guba, 1985). It is also possible, and perhaps probable, that these parallel criteria were advanced because many qualitative research scholars were, to some degree, still impelled by a residual belief in objectivity—at least in some form. Transcending the assumptions of the dominant framework is far and away no easy task, particularly for those in the forefront of such an immense paradigm shift. For qualitative research scholars, this impulse translated into the development of procedures thought to be capable of at least reigning in what they saw as the most troubling intrusions of researcher subjectivity.

It was in the midst of these paradigm debates that I completed a doctoral program that centered on the scientific method. Although I was supported in my choice to conduct a qualitative dissertation, my study was done at the time that qualitative inquiry was rapidly coming to be viewed as alternative set of methods with the same quantitative research goal of prediction and control. I was expected to employ these methods and criteria; and, dutifully attempting compliance I soldiered on with determination. Very quickly, however, found the situation completely untenable, and that in turn led me to seriously question this approach. As I continued my interest, I read widely the work of philosophers and educational researchers who pushed past alternative methods to an entirely different understanding of epistemology and ontology.

My explorations brought me to the work of Lous Heshusius, whose scholarship has led to some of the most intellectually important ideas about an alternative understanding of educational inquiry and disability studies/critical special education. Not that she achieved immediate acceptance among researchers and teachers. Her ideas have been too original—too unapologetically nonconforming in ways that deftly permeate well beyond the surface of

THE ILLUSION OF OUR SEPARATIVENESS 77

the subject matter at hand. Not unexpectedly, those who are quite satisfied with (and invested in) the institutionally established ways of doing and thinking find Heshusius' work decidedly unappealing. It has just the opposite effect on those who are searching, or who have searched, for more morally satisfying answers.

2   Heshusuius—On Freeing Ourselves from Objectivity

When the editors of this volume invited my contribution, I thought immediately of Heshusius. Among all of her work, the totality of which has influenced me profoundly, Heshusius' (1994) article, *Freeing Ourselves from Objectivity: Managing Subjectivity or Turning Toward a Participatory Mode of Consciousness*, is the one that strikes the deepest chord. I am sure that I have read it dozens of times, and it is by far the only article by *anyone* that I have read and re-read so many times. Each time I have returned to it over the years, I realize all over again how intensely it spoke to me on my first reading of it, and how completely it has affected me not only on the professional level but in so many aspects of my life.

Here Heshusius might well point out that I am being superfluous by invoking such a separation between the professional and the personal, and no doubt I am. And so, just for the sake of organization and for that sake only, I will first attempt to trace out what this piece of work has imparted in terms of leading me to a coherent sense of what research, and especially disability research, is all about. Little did I realize that in the process it has affected my entire sense of what it means to simply to *be*—in every sense of the word. I'll turn my attention to this most pivotal issue second, keeping in mind that the "research" and "being" issues cannot at all be disentangled.

In, *Freeing Ourselves from Objectivity*, Heshusius opposed the presumptions of the then recently popularized methods for managing researcher "subjectivity," pointing out that such attempts at controlling and regulating research may appeal as a seemingly desirable way of engaging in full disclosure of one's subjectivity, if not purging or sanitizing research of idiosyncratic prejudices. Early on, I recognized (at least on an articulate level) *only* that this work illuminated my path through the thickets of methodological perplexity. How was I to negotiate the many conflicting accounts of how qualitative research is properly conducted? Most specifically, what was there to do with the left over baggage of all those injunctions to strive for at least some version of methodological objectivity?

By the time I read *Freeing Ourselves from Objectivity*, I had, or thought I had, dispensed with that baggage. But when attempting to explain my indifference toward concerns for objectivity of some type to ardent colleagues, I found myself dithering over why (exactly) I found it to be such a pointless endeavor. I had already written but not yet published a piece about my very early experiences with the absurdities of attempting to use procedures to manage my own subjectivity in the process of researching novice special education teachers (Gallagher, 1995); yet, a fully coherent philosophical explanation for why it is absurd still eluded me. I just didn't have a coherent account to offer to incredulous others who marveled at my indifference. Heshusius provided a better approach.

Sometimes it is better to ask questions than offer answers; and she has a way of asking devastatingly good questions, as in the following salvo on the notion of managing subjectivity:

> A long list of questions comes to mind when I read about the need for researchers to manage their subjectivity. When researchers tell us (or themselves), here are the subjective parts of me that were involved in the research process, shouldn't they also be able to state what parts were not subjective? *Are* there parts of us that are not subjective? If so, are the not-subjective parts objective? If that is the case, then are we able to be objective after all, after we thought we had done away with it? If so, must I then assume that we have a reliable and/or objective way of knowing our subjectivity? The idea seems to be that we can construct what we call "subjectivity" as something we can be in charge of by the sheer force of trying to restrain "it," account for "it," and keep "it" under our management. (p. 16, emphasis in original)

My initial response to encountering this passage for the first time was one of mirthful relief, which soon gave way to silent gratitude. There. She had done it. She had completely shattered the constraining artificialities of *subjectivity management* I found so troubling. Really, it is eloquent in its simplicity—without objectivity there can be no subjectivity. One defines the other, and in the absence of being able to *objectively* know *about our subjectivity*, the terms become meaningless.

In reading, *Freeing Ourselves from Objectivity*, I came also to realize that there is much more to the desire for separation, for abstracting and distancing ourselves as researchers, or educators, or, ultimately, as human beings, than meets the eye. Such striving for separation, she pointed out, is not without its consequences because it inescapably leads to a deep sense of alienation. "For most of human history," she noted,

> humans did not know objectively, and therefore did not know subjectively as we presently use the term. The belief that one can actually dis-

THE ILLUSION OF OUR SEPARATIVENESS 79

tance oneself, and then regulate that distance in order to come to know, has also been referred to as alienated consciousness, as the disenchantment of knowing, a mode of consciousness that has led to undreamed of technological advances, but has also left us alienated from each other, from nature, and from ourselves. (p. 16)

It would be one thing if this alienation were simply the price that must be paid for the production of valuable knowledge or effective teaching practices. If that were the case, the only question would be whether we have paid too much for all of our advances; but, that is not all there is to the story. Instead, this alienated mode of consciousness leads to ways of knowing that can be, and often are, quite damaging and distorting.

Prior to having read *Freeing Ourselves from Objectivity*, it had never occurred to me that Western philosophy's dualism—the creation of the opposing concepts of objective and subjective as distinctive ways of knowing, the separation of the mind from the body, and so on—might be intimately connected not only to our mistaken notions of research objectivity and subjectivity, but also to our ecological crisis that is growing worse by the day. Citing Evernden (1985), Heshusius made this connection unambiguous:

The crisis is the externalization of the distancing, alienated mode of consciousness we have chosen to live within. We do not have an objective relationship to the planet (as the scientific revolution would have it), nor do we have a subjective relationship to the planet (as sentimental discussions about the ecology would have it). Either conception of the self-planet relationship shields us from having to face the crisis as being identical to the nature of our chosen mode of consciousness. Concerns around procedural objectivity and subjectivity in educational research mirror, I believe, a similar misunderstanding: They do not in their essential meaning refer to methodological problems. They point to how we understand the nature of our consciousness. (p. 17)

These connections prompted me to consider the possible connections between this alienated mode of consciousness and the rampant ethos of individualism, exploitation, competition, and cult of personality that increasingly dominates contemporary culture across the globe.

Further, she pointed out that such distancing makes sense if the intention is to exert control over others. Accordingly, in order to experience superiority of knowledge and the power that comes with it, the other must first be constructed as separate from the self. While it is fairly obvious why this act of distancing alienates us from our fellow human beings (it's hard to have authentic relationship with those we objectify), the thought that it leads to alienation from oneself was one I found intriguing. It seems as if the opposite would be true. To become individuated or separate would seem to suggest a self-sufficiency or self-coherence that essentially precluded this kind of alienation.

Very much to the contrary, Heshusius wrote of how the act of self-distancing in the pursuit of knowledge and control leaves us alienated and disenchanted because it denies us the wholeness that comes from being connected, having a "kinship" with who and what we come to know. Imposing separation, or creating what she referred to as the "experience of 'I' as separate from the world" serves to "block full perception of the other" (p. 16). Her point here can be summarized as—to be human is to be connected, not only to one another, but also to non-human others and to the natural world. Without those connections, we can't know who we are any more than we can come to know who others are.

This concept of kinship and connection as essential for wholeness was one that has stayed with me. It is also one I found echoed in the work of several philosophers who have explored the nature of the "self." For example, in *Sources of the Self*, Charles Taylor (1989) posed the point that what we know as the self is conceived and forged through relationships with others within the contingencies of the social, cultural, and historical contexts. Put another way, being a self is communal project. Each of us is only *someone* in relation to who we are to others. In speaking to the unassailable fact of our interdependency with one another, MacIntyre (1999) asserted that, "… our self-knowledge too depends in key part upon what we learn about ourselves from others, and more than this, upon a confirmation of our own judgments about ourselves by others who know us well, a confirmation that only such others can provide" (p. 94). And along the same lines, Sandel (1998) critiqued the theory of the individual self as existing prior to and holding a distinct status apart from its bonds to others, effectively contending that there is no such thing as the "antecedently individuated" self (p. 64). Because this concept of the self denies our interconnectedness and interdependencies, it fundamentally misrepresents who we are as human beings and thus denies us the experience of wholeness.

"The question becomes" Heshusius told us, " whether we accept individuation, individuality, and independent identity as the starting ground for inquiry (characterizations of the self-other relationship fundamental to the Western mindset), or whether we understand the concept of self as epistemically related to other through self-other unity" (p. 17). What does it mean to be epistemically related to other—and how do we engage in self-other unity?

THE ILLUSION OF OUR SEPARATIVENESS

3   Turning toward Participatory Consciousness

The clear and, may I say lovely, answer she offered us is that we come to know by transcending our self-imposed separation from others, from the world, and from nature through what she conceived of as "participatory consciousness"—"an inner desire to let go of perceived boundaries that constitute '*self*,'" and "a temporary eclipse of all the perceiver's egocentric thoughts and strivings, of all preoccupations with self and self-esteem" (p. 16). "This temporary self-forgetfulness is not to be equated with loss of self," she added, "but points to the possibility of fundamental *selfother* unity in which egocentric thoughts, feelings, and needs are voluntarily released" (p. 16).

As one continues to read it becomes clear that it is not a matter of slipping in and out of egocentrism, as in forcing ourselves to become temporarily better people. Rather, it is that an "individual" is no more authentically herself when she has forgotten about her[self] by becoming so captivated (in her words, "enchanted") with the other that egocentrism recedes, thus allowing to arise the connection that was there all along. "Participatory consciousness," she explained, "is the awareness of a deeper level of kinship between the knower and the known" (p. 16), and "involves letting go of the idea of being-separate-and-in-charge altogether" (p. 18). Not that this letting go is easy to accomplish.

In a particularly illuminating example of a researcher's attempt at letting go of the need to be *in charge* without attempting to manage her *subjectivity*, Heshusius related Fujita's (1990) account of her efforts to undertake research with, as Heshusius described him, "a very different and difficult [for the researcher] other" (p. 19) who essentially ignored Fujita's overtures. After exhausting her efforts to engage the young man in conversation as he remained preoccupied with his fingers held above his head, she finally lies down next to him and engages in the same activity. Her description of what transpired is worth quoting from Heshusius' article here:

> This is interesting, I think. "Is this how you do it, Matt?" I ask Matthew, who has a glimpse of me and goes back to his finger play again, without showing any interest in what I am doing. I continue to flick my fingers for a while. "Don't you think I am doing well?" I ask him again, which receives the same lack of reaction from him. I feel uneasy about his ignoring me this time. (p. 60)

And in another highly evocative example, Heshusius recounted a year-long participant observation she undertook in a group home with people who were, at that time, labeled as "retarded" (Heshusius, 1981). As the researcher and as someone who did not experience having this egregiously stigmatizing label, she was blocked from fully attending by her keen awareness of the power and status disparities between the other participants and herself.

> I was forced to recognize my upbringing, values, and related emotions until I finally came to pose the question of merging: Could I imagine such a life for myself? Only when I could start seeing their lives as worthy of myself, or for my children, could I extend myself somatically, forget the ego concerns that constitute the self, and be fully attentive. (p. 19)

Instead of needing to get rid of or trying to subjugate our values and beliefs (as if that were possible), Heshusius clarified that by attending to them, by noticing them non-judgmentally, our values and beliefs make access possible.

When a short time later I read Gadamer's (1975) critique of our "prejudice against prejudice" I recognized its resonance with Heshusius' insight that our feelings and values are indispensable to knowing. And so she takes us beyond dichotomy, showing that in participatory consciousness, "[r]eality is no longer understood as truth to be interpreted but as mutually evolving" (p. 18). She then followed with what I found to be one of the most clarifying insights I have encountered:

> Participatory consciousness, then, does not stand in opposition to the concepts of objectivity and subjectivity: It simply effaces them. There-fore, the possibility and nature of participatory consciousness cannot be evaluated from within the objectivity-subjectivity dualism. (p. 18)

> To ask about how to achieve research objectivity or the management of researcher subjectivity is simply to ask the wrong question. Further, the question is not about what methods do, but what we think we were doing with the methods.

> As she went on to elaborate, knowing *objectively* is *not*, in any event, how we as human beings *know* the world, each other, or ourselves. "Don't we reach out, (whether we are aware of it or not)" she asked, "to what we want to know *with* all of ourselves, because we can't do anything else?" (p. 16, italics in original)

I believe Heshusius' concept of participatory consciousness was, and is, far ahead of its time. And I am sure that it hasn't received the recognition its

THE ILLUSION OF OUR SEPARATIVENESS 83

brilliance deserves. After all, "researchers" don't engage in talk about "enchant-ment" or "kinship" or "forgetting the self." I can, however, wryly envision a roomful of corporate technology entrepreneurs hearing the phrase "participa-tory consciousness" and nearly jumping out of their seats to ask, "Is this a new kind of virtual communication! And can we make a profit on this?" But they would be missing the point, wouldn't they?

Embedded in Heshusius' concept of participatory consciousness is the understanding that all knowledge is moral. Reversing the old adage that "knowledge is power," she shared another epiphany that occurred when she was researching in the group home. It was only when she realized that authen-tic awareness could only occur when she entered into a state of relatedness with them. "When one forgets self and becomes embedded in what one wants to understand," she concluded, "there is an affirmative quality of kinship that no longer allows for privileged status. *It renders the act of knowing an ethical act*" (p. 19, emphasis added).

This brings me to the personal impact this piece. It introduced to me for the first time the understanding that, as the eastern philosophers I have since read put it, we are all *dependent arisings*. The very notion that there is a sep-arate "self" beyond outward form is itself an illusion. Our very connectedness and interdependency leaves no room for concerns of hierarchy or invidious comparison. This understanding is by far the most liberatory and meaningful insights I have ever received. I am still in the process of trying to realize it's the full implications.

4   Participatory Consciousness in the Inclusive Classroom

When we engage in the act of research, we are seeking to make sense of the world—or at least the part of the world that captures our interests. We "reach out," as Heshusius put it, "to what we want to know *with* all of ourselves ... because we can't do anything else" (p. 16). *All of ourselves* includes the qualities (such as beliefs, values, experiences, and intentions) that make us human and are the reasons we want to know in the first place. But these qualities have also come to be viewed as a source of discomfort in that they confront us with the limitations of our knowledge—the inability, as Schwandt (1996, p. 59) put it, to secure "final vindication" for our choices and actions. So instead we look to method as a bulwark against the possibility that our beliefs might be errone-ous, the existential fear that our values might be inappropriate or even con-temptible, and the often tacit desire to leave our intentions unexamined lest they reveal something we'd rather not acknowledge.

In precisely the same way, educators look to method to shield us from the threat of failure and feelings of incompetency. If someone can just provide a set of teaching methods will guarantee that they will get it right, tell them what to do so as to provide the very best for students, then they can rest assured that they are doing their best. Classroom teachers have been told by those who apparently know more that only teaching methods based on objective "scientific" research, the ones called "evidence-based," can deliver on this promise. Wouldn't it be irresponsible not to use them?

And so, dutifully, they submit. If they find that teaching becomes a stultifying routine of forcing students, some more willing than others, through a relentless series of mechanistic tasks, then that is simply what must be done. The same alienated consciousness between the knower and the known that Heshusius described in objectivist research becomes the alienated consciousness between teachers and their students. The same distancing and ensuing sense of separation ultimately turns to disenchantment when teaching becomes a matter of doing things *to* students rather than engaging *with* students. Students, inexplicably it seems, also experience disenchantment with learning. And if some students fail to measure up, *the problem* must be within them—presumably due to a disability or some other less formalized shortcoming. Something, presumably a more intense version of this method-driven teaching pattern, must be done to manage and remediate their deficiencies.

This approach to teaching and learning creates educational and social exclusion because it cannot do otherwise. And it should be no wonder that attempts to achieve inclusive education under the same circumstances cannot be anything other than ineffectual. Further, one does not have to speculate much about why research-proven and methods-driven discussions about how to achieve inclusion tend to go nowhere. So why do we continue with this approach?

Perhaps it is because it is hard to live with uncertainty and all of the vulnerabilities that it entails. Why wouldn't it be better to use method as a way out? In *Freeing Ourselves from Objectivity*, Heshusius made it clear that there is no way out—not through method, not through a misplaced allegiance to research objectivity, and not even through attempts to manage research subjectivity. Instead, she prompted us to consider that transcendence comes through not only accepting but embracing our human limitations and entering a participatory mode of consciousness. Such a move involves learning to acknowledge our fears and uncertainties, as Heshusius put it, without judgment or self-condemnation, and then let go of them. It also involves a willingness to risk an honest appraisal of our beliefs, values, and intentions.

Entering into a participatory mode of consciousness in the classroom means that teaching is no longer methods-driven. Here I must emphasize that this does not mean that teachers don't use methods, but rather that methods are not used as a substitute for genuine social, emotional and intellectual engagement with students. Teaching is the act of participation, of co-constructing knowledge with students.

By illustration, during a discussion about inclusive teaching in a seminar class I taught, one graduate student who was also an experienced teacher shared a marvelous epiphany with the class. "I have spent my whole career looking for just the right methods that would get my students to achieve their learning goals," she stated. "And until this very moment, I never realized that teaching comes from within me." I should add that she shared this realization with an expression of true relief on her face—as though she realized that she was suddenly free to connect with her students, to be authentic, and in essence to be herself. Suddenly, the classroom became a place where teachers and students make sense of things together.

Extending Heshusius' concept of participatory consciousness allows us to consider that inclusion, like research or inquiry, is a way of being—not a way of doing. When approached this way, the *how* of doing follows the *why* of doing. Inclusive education becomes an ethical act, and can only be talked about—and enacted—in those terms. This enactment of participatory consciousness unavoidably involves taking some personal risks—of failing at times, of having to confront ourselves in uncomfortable ways, and of honest exposure and appraisal our values on the part of both ourselves and others.

Acknowledgement

This chapter originally appeared as Gallagher, D. (2015). The illusion of our separativeness: Exploring Heshusius' concept of participatory consciousness in disability research and inclusive education. In *Foundations of Inclusive Education Research* (pp. 205–221) (International Perspectives on Inclusive Education, Vol. 6). Emerald Group Publishing Limited (https://doi.org/10.1108/S1479-363620150000006011). Reprinted here with permission from Emerald Group Publishing Limited.

Note

1   Interested readers will certainly want to read Dianne Ferguson and Phil Ferguson's (2000) highly engaging article on the distorting effects of imposing objectivist procedural criteria on qualitative research in the professional review process.

References

Bernstein, R. (1983). *Beyond objectivism and relativism: Science, hermeneutics, and praxis*. Philadelphia, PA: University of Pennsylvania Press.

Bogdan, R., & Biklen, S. (1982). *Qualitative research for education: An introduction to theory and practice*. New York, NY: Allyn and Bacon Inc.

Dewey, J. (1916). *Democracy and education*. New York, NY: Macmillan.

Dewey, J. (1938). *Experience and education*. Toronto: Collier-MacMillan Canada Ltd.

Eisner, E. W., & Peshkin, A. (Eds.). (1990). *Qualitative inquiry in education: The continuing debate*. New York, NY: Teachers College Press.

Evernden, N. (1985). *The natural alien: Humankind and environment*. Toronto: University of Toronto Press.

Ferguson, D. L., & Ferguson, P. M. (2000). Qualitative research in special education: Notes toward an open inquiry instead of a new orthodoxy? *Journal of the Association for Persons with Severe Handicaps, 25*(3), 180–185.

Fujita, C. (1990). *Understanding lifeworlds of mentally handicapped children* (Unpublished doctoral dissertation). Department of Secondary Education, University of Alberta, Alberta.

Gadamer, H.-G. (1975). *Truth and method* (G. Barden & J. Cumming, Eds. & Trans.). New York, NY: Seabury Press.

Gage, N. L. (1978). *The scientific basis of the art of teaching*. Oxford: Teachers College Press.

Gage, N. L. (1989). The paradigm wars and their aftermath: A "historical" sketch of research on teaching since 1989. *Educational Researcher, 18*(7), 4–10.

Gallagher, D. J. (1995). In search of the rightful role of method: Reflections on my dissertation experience. In T. Tiller, A. Sparkes, S. Karhus, & F. Dowling-Naess (Eds.), *Reflections on educational research: The qualitative challenge* (pp. 25–42). Bergen: Kasper Forlag.

Gallagher, D. J. (2006). If not absolute objectivity, then what? A reply to Kauffman and Sasso. *Exceptionality, 14*(2), 91–107.

Guba, E. (1981). Criteria for assessing the trustworthiness of naturalistic inquiry. *Educational Communication and Technology Journal, 29*, 79–92.

Hanson, N. (1958). *Patterns of discovery*. Cambridge: Cambridge University Press.

Heshusius, L. (1981). *Meaning in life as experienced by persons labeled retarded in a group home: A participant observation study*. Springfield, IL: Charles Thomas.

Heshusius, L. (1986). Paradigm shifts and special education: A response to Ulman and Rosenberg. *Exceptional Children, 52*(5), 461–465.

Heshusius, L. (1989). The Newtonian mechanistic paradigm, special education, and contours of alternatives: An overview. *Journal of Learning Disabilities, 22*(7), 403–415.

THE ILLUSION OF OUR SEPARATIVENESS 87

Heshusius, L. (1994). Freeing ourselves from objectivity: Managing subjectivity or turning toward a participatory mode of consciousness. *Educational Researcher, 23*(3), 15–22.

Iano, R. P. (1986). The study and development of teaching: With implications for the advancement of special education. *Remedial and Special Education, 7*(5), 50–61.

Kauffman, J. M. (1987). Research in special education a commentary. *Remedial and Special Education, 8*(6), 57–62.

Kuhn, T. (1962). *The structure of scientific revolutions.* Chicago, IL: University of Chicago Press.

Lincoln, Y. S., & Guba, E. G. (1985). *Naturalistic inquiry.* Newbury Park: CA: Sage.

MacIntyre, A. (1999). *Dependent rational animals: Why human beings need virtues.* London: Duckworth.

Miles, M., & Huberman, A. (1984). Drawing valid meaning from qualitative data: Toward a shared craft. *Educational Researcher, 13*(5), 20–30.

Nagel, T. (1986). *The view from nowhere.* New York, NY: Oxford University Press.

Phillips, D. C. (1987). *Philosophy, science and social inquiry: Contemporary methodological controversies in social science and related applied fields of research.* Oxford: Pergamon Press.

Poplin, M. S. (1987). Self-imposed blindness: The scientific method in education. *Remedial and Special Education, 8*(6), 31–37.

Porter, T. M. (1995). *Trust in numbers: The pursuit of objectivity in science and public life.* Princeton, NJ: Princeton University Press.

Putnam, H. (1981). *Reason, truth, and history.* Cambridge: Cambridge University Press.

Rorty, R. (1979). *Philosophy and the mirror of nature.* Princeton, NJ: Princeton University Press.

Sandel, M. (1998). *Liberalism and the limits of justice* (2nd ed.). Cambridge: Cambridge University Press.

Schwandt, T. A. (1980). *Some consequences of the value-free claim for the conduct of inquiry* (Unpublished qualifying paper). Inquiry Methodology, School of Education, Indiana University, Bloomington, IN.

Schwandt, T. A. (1996). Farewell to criteriology. *Qualitative Inquiry, 2*, 58–72.

Schwandt, T. R. (1990). Paths to inquiry in the social disciplines: Scientific, constructivist, and critical theory methodologies. In E. G. Guba (Ed.), *The paradigm dialog* (pp. 258–276). Newbury Park/London/Delhi: International Professional Publishers.

Skrtic, T. M. (1986). The crisis in special education knowledge: A perspective on perspective. *Focus on Exceptional Children, 18*(7), 1–16.

Skrtic, T. M. (1991). *Behind special education: A critical analysis of professional culture and school organization.* Denver, CO: Love Publishing Company.

Slavin, R. E. (2002). Evidence-based education policies: Transforming education practice and research. *Educational Researcher, 31*(7), 15–21.

Smith, J. K. (1983). Quantitative versus qualitative research: An attempt to clarify the issue. *Educational Researcher, 12*(3), 6–13.

Smith, J. K. (1989). *The nature of social and educational inquiry: Empiricism versus interpretation.* New York, NY: Ablex Publishing Corporation.

Smith, J. K., & Heshusius, L. (1986). Closing down the conversation: The end of the quantitative-qualitative debate among educational inquirers. *Educational Researcher, 15*(1), 4–12.

Stanovich, K. E. (1990). A call for an end to the paradigm wars in reading research. *Journal of Literacy Research, 22*(3), 221–231.

Taylor, C. (1989). *Sources of the self: The making of the modern identity.* Cambridge, MA: Harvard University Press.

CHAPTER 6

Respect for the Ghost, Justice for the Living: A Sociological Haunting 30 Years in the Making

Danielle M. Cowley

Abstract

This chapter concludes with Cowley's reflexivity in the form of a letter to Heshusius, seeking resolution to threads that were left unwoven in the narrative research Cowley conducted for her doctoral research. Decades separate their research, yet. Heshusius' insights and connections to the present make for a powerful argument for this series, to suggest the relevance of returning to the founding voices of critical special educators who made possible, the evolution of disability studies in education.

Keywords

isolation – autonomy – identity – advocacy – narrative research

1 Introduction

During my years as a graduate student in special education, one aspect of the coursework and the literature my fellow students and I were exposed to, became increasingly bothersome to me, to the point of becoming intolerable. This was the virtual absence of the voices of the people most involved—the exceptional persons themselves. While examining theories, positions, and research findings that reflected what we, the professionals, thought should be done and how we should do it, they, the persons we had labeled this way or that, were rarely asked what they thought about their own matters. (Heshusius, 1981, p. v)

© KONINKLIJKE BRILL NV, LEIDEN, 2020 | DOI: 10.1163/9789004427280_007

Dear Lous,[1]

As a recently appointed Assistant Professor at the University of Northern Iowa, I was honored and overwhelmed at the invitation to write this chapter. My junior rank in the field of Disability Studies in Education meant that your book, *Challenging Orthodoxy in Special Education: Dissenting Voices* (Gallagher, Heshusius, Iano, & Skrtic, 2003) was required reading during my doctoral studies. A librarian would look in shame at my dog-eared, broken-binding edition of this seminal text. It is fortuitous that I remain to this day, living in the land of dissenting voices as I teach, engage in research, and write with your former colleagues.

So, when I was invited to consider my work against your 1981 book, *Meaning in Life as Experienced by Persons Labeled Retarded in a Group Home: A Participant Observation Study*, I replied, "of course!" Although I did not own a copy, I found your well-worn evergreen, hardcover with yellowed pages in the basement of our university's library. It had that pleasant, aromatic smell of old books: oily, woody, and musty letting me know of the timeless secrets it held. When I read the first paragraph of your preface, I had to read it a second time. Lingering over the pages I paused and flipped back to the copyright, yes, 1981. While reading your long-since-published book I felt immediately transported, not only back in time to 1981, but to a time five years past when I began eerily similar research of my own (Cowley, 2013). I was immediately alerted to a distinct structure of feeling—to the experience of being in that time, nearly forty years ago and being in a more recent time, five years ago as I completed my research. And at once, I was haunted by this realization.

The dark, windowless library basement, the musty smell of your book, and even the recognition that you probably walked the halls of this same basement created a ghostly matter (Gordon, 2008). But, this ghostly matter wasn't about some bothersome ghoul lurking under the stairs. This haunting was "tied to historical and social effects" (Gordon, 2008, p. 190). It was a reminder how history makes social life, and made plain the ways in which ableism is historically imbedded in our society. While reading your book, the participants (the lived) met me (the living) and they demanded a reckoning. My intensions with this letter are to show the similar ways in which both our pieces of work exposed the cracks and rigging of special education and disability services. Both pieces helped "the people who are meant to be invisible show up" (Gordon, 2008, p. xvi). I also wanted to share with you my disturbed feelings that cannot and will not be put away, at least until something different is done on behalf of the young people we both describe in our research.

My dissertation explored the lives of young women with disability labels, one of whom lived in a group home, all of whom experienced segregation, exclusion, and various denials of personhood. Our work offers a close study of unresolved social violence against disabled youth. Many attitudes, beliefs, practices, and experiences have not changed over the past 40 years as too often people with intellectual disabilities are presumed to lack competence. Claims to disabled sexuality are shifting, shaped by an exciting wave of redefinition, but sex education remains woefully absent in today's schools. And although sheltered "work" is finally being dismantled across the U.S., inclusive, competitive employment remains out of reach for many. Echoes of violence linger in the everyday lives of disabled youth. Finally, too, those bothersome and intolerable professionals you mentioned were still were taking up the same epistemological space in my research. The social violence hasn't stopped. I remember writing the literature review for my dissertation and as you noted, I too became incensed over the missing voices of "exceptional persons themselves" (Hesushius, 1981, p. v). Today, only a handful of professionals still decide to actually invite young people to talk about their lives and the choices, or lack thereof, they make about those lives. I would personally classify the majority of these professionals, who actually go to young people, as dissenters. I am sure you would agree.

And I became angry with this and wondered, "Would this anger cloud my analysis?" "Would I become too emotional when conducting this research?" DeVault (1999) assured me that to become angry at what we are experiencing and learning as qualitative researchers was not uncommon. She encourages researchers challenge "the right of the powerful to define realities for us all" (p. 1) by resisting authorized knowledge production that ignores the experiences, stories, and perspectives of women—in the case of my work, young women with disabilities. The excavation of women's experiences ignites a journey "to find what has been ignored, censored, and suppressed, and to reveal both the diversity of actual women's lives and the ideological mechanisms that have made so many of those lives invisible" (DeVault, 1999, p. 32).

I was also reading work by Dorothy Smith (2005), Susan Wendell (1996; 2006), Scot Danforth and Susan Gabel (2006), Patricia Clough (1994), and Sharlene Nagy Hesse-Biber (2007). These authors were critiquing dominant avenues of patriarchal knowledge production. They advocated for changes in status, subverted authorial knowledge claims made by those in positions of power, and called for social justice. They were all just as angry as I was. So I crumpled up that "memo to self" and threw it away. I made an active commitment to justice for the living. I embraced my emotionality.

What is research with humans if emotion is not involved? My anger toward those who sidelined the knowledge of adolescents with disabilities or who attempted to make claims about their lives without ever speaking to an actual disabled student, strengthened my resolve when asked the very reasonable question by others, "have you considered speaking with the participants' parents or teachers?" I never regretted my gut reaction in response to those questions as a declared the parameters of my research.

1. No I will not interview teachers.
2. No I will not interview parents or guardians.
3. No I will not triangulate my data against the perceptions of adults.
4. No I will not render these young women voiceless.

1.1 *Coding Daily Injustices*

I knew this stance was grounded in emotions I could not name. Yet, soon enough, while I was coding a conversation between a participant, Hope[2] and myself, emotion gave way to clear injustice. How does a researcher code a conversation with a 21-year-old who shares her dreams of attending a culinary arts program, but who's lived reality indicates that the closest she has come to culinary arts is stirring juice in the kitchen of her group home while getting ready to leave for a tour of the sheltered workshop? Here is what the analytical task of coding looked like when faced with the structural oppression experienced by Hope: interests, daily activities, careers, post-secondary education, sheltered work, dream discrepancies, economic disparity, access to opportunity, consequences of labeling, segregation, racial inequity, intersectionality, ableism, institutional oppression.

So much of my coding throughout my data analysis process presented a messy collision of the seemingly mundane (i.e., interests and daily activities) with the oppressive (economic disparity, access to opportunity, consequences of labeling, racial inequity). This is what happens when you pay attention to your emotionality and ground the complex analytical task of coding in critical methodologies—methodologies outlined by authors such as Mertens (2005) who explicitly recognizes that gender discrimination is systemic and structural, and that research is political, or Creswell and Pano-Clark (2011) who encourage emancipatory theoretical lenses and social change, or Charmaz (2006) who extends grounded theory to the social justice arena by asking, "what might [these stories] suggest about social justice?" (p. 517).

But no theory or analytical framework can quite prepare a researcher for the emotional materiality involved when coding such specific instances of a young, disabled, African-American woman constrained within an ableist

RESPECT FOR THE GHOST, JUSTICE FOR THE LIVING

system that has determined sheltered work is a reasonable post-school outcome for her. I am sure you, Lous, experienced similar feelings during your study. My emotional materiality was tears. I cried when I transcribed Hope's story, I cried when I coded it, and I cried during my dissertation defense. Yet, we know that such conversations capture but a sliver of the discrepancies between the dreams and the realities for many disabled youth. My data captured just a sliver of the decisions made *for* my participants rather than *by* them. And in truth, my dissertation captured just a sliver of the oppression young people with disabilities face everyday. So actually, who am I to cry? It would seem, that you, Lous, may have felt an emotional entanglement in 1981, when you asked: "Why do we more often than not stand in the way of these persons' search for more meaningful living?" (p. vii).

1.2 *Research to Practice*

Hope's story irrevocably changed my approach to preparing teachers. I now teach several courses related to transition and coordinate the *Transition Programming for College and Careers* emphasis for my university's Master of Education in Special Education. My conversations with Hope playback many times in my head and I share the emotionality with my students. I tell my pre-service teachers that sheltered work is absolutely, unequivocally an option for *no one*. I share no gray area with them and I am firm when the question arises, "Yeah, but what about this student?" Instead, my students must visit and reflect upon various employment settings that offer post-secondary, and community-access services and supports for young adults with disabilities. If they visit an agency that engages in "piece-rate work" they must reflect through a *critical* lens. My course also invites consideration of possible options for college, careers, and community engagement. Hope and so many other disabled youth haunt me in such a powerful way that I could never imagine not teaching for justice—that is—not teaching for inclusive living and life-long learning. The ghosts and the harm inflicted upon them by social violence won't allow it. Sheltered work is one damaging piece of history woven through both our studies.

Independence, romantic relationships, and understandings of the self were three themes examined in your study that reached across into mine. In the sections that follow, I share our participants' stories related these themes, but I also unpack them for any social and material violence that remains. In doing so, I hope to create a hospitable place for the ghosts, while remaining partial to the living; to make the past memorable, but the future imaginable; and to make the symptoms of troubles visible, while speaking to justice and transformation.

2 Introducing the Participants across Time

When you introduced me, and all your other readers, to the participants in your study I became ever more certain that Gordon's (2008) ghosts and hauntings were at play. Ghosts are not simply dead or missing people. It is very likely that many of your participants are alive to this day. But by investigating ghostly narratives we are forced to remember the state-sanctioned terrors of the eugenics movement and the criminalization, euthanasia, sterilization, and institutionalization of the disabled. Through remembering we make visible the lingering effects of such violence: the pressures of prenatal testing, the resurgence of right-to-die narratives, segregated schooling, sheltered work, and the school-to-prison pipeline. As Gordon (2008) writes,

> The ghost or apparition is one form by which something lost, or barely visible, or seemingly not there to our supposedly well-trained eyes, makes itself known or apparent to us, in its own way of course. The way of the ghost is haunting, and haunting is a particular way of knowing what has happened or what is happening. Being haunted draws us affectively, sometimes against our will and always a bit magically, into the structure of feeling of a reality we come to experience, not as cold knowledge, but as a transformative recognition. (p. 8)

I was immediately, affectively, magically drawn to your participants and their stories. Eight people labeled "mentally retarded" (in the vernacular of that time) all living together in a group home. Pam and Kitty, who spent much of their day in a sheltered workshop, reminded me again of Hope who was 21-years-old when I met her. She was a young Black woman labeled with an intellectual disability, who received free and/or reduced lunch at school. She had cerebral palsy, used a manual wheelchair, and struggled with verbal communication. Unfortunately the special education and service delivery systems of today respond to these intersections of race, class, gender, and disability by segregating Hope. Similar to the participants from your 1981 study: she lived in a group home with five housemates (most of whom were at least twenty years older than she), attended segregated special education classes, and was slotted to begin sheltered work a few months after I finished my study. Hope reminds us of the dire circumstances of an institutionalized life than remains unchanged for far too many disabled youth today.

Staff members constructed some participants in your study, like Lisa and Rob, as more competent and capable of greater independent living conditions. It's remarkable how much power a staff member can have in determining the

RESPECT FOR THE GHOST, JUSTICE FOR THE LIVING

humanness and potential in another (Blatt, 1977). Others, like Max and Don, struggled with the structure of group home living, where you could never truly be alone and others constantly harassed you. Then there was Terry, who expressed countless times her desire for a home, friends, and boyfriends. Your haunting descriptions of people longing for a future different than the present and of pushing back against structures that limited choice and independence, made even more clear to me how powerfully alive disability oppression remains tethered to "institutional ableism" (Beratan, 2006).

Reading your descriptions remind me of Victoria, another participant from my study who talked often of friends and her boyfriend. Victoria was soft-spoken, polite, and labeled intellectually disabled (Down Sydrome). Her White, upper-middle socio-economic background afforded her the cultural and financial capital to push back against systems that would attempt to stifle her. When I first met Victoria she was sixteen-years-old and had just filmed a public service advertisement (PSA) in New York City for an anti-bullying campaign to end the use of the R-word ("retarded"). She was in ninth grade during the time of my study and attended some regular education classrooms, but her primary educational setting was the segregated special education classroom. She was actively involved in the local Special Olympics; loved all things related to Disney and "tween"-pop culture; and on the weekends she hung out with friends who participated in cheerleading with her. Victoria enjoyed talking on the phone to her boyfriend after school, going out to eat at local restaurants, and speaking to her imaginary friends.

When reading your account of Terry and her desire for friends and boyfriends, Victoria kept interrupting my thoughts. I returned to Victoria's narrative in my study and I became preoccupied with the memory of Terry as you portrayed her. Thirty years ago, five years ago, I pictured Victoria and Terry as real friends, texting each other today about their dreams of boyfriends, marriage, and (imaginary) friends. Imaginary friends? Invisible friends occurring in my imagination, or as the ghosts recounted by Gordon (2008) in his *Ghostly Matters: Hauntings and the Sociological Imagination*? You see, Lous, all of your participants made visible the echoes of social violence that lingers in the lives of today's disabled youth. Your participants forced me to a confrontation by making it so clear that the seemingly "over-and-done-with [has come] alive" (Gordon, 2008, p. xvi). The ways in which three particular themes from your study (independence, romantic relationships, and understandings of the self) remain a part of history, but they also live quite vibrantly and *violently* in the present. The damage done by segregated living, working, and learning is done and the violence remains, but as you will see new and different futures are beginning—the ghosts are forcing a reckoning.

3 A Conversation on Independence

The participants from your study voiced such deep concerns and desires for independence because their lives were entrenched in institutionalization (Goffman, 1963). They may not have lived in an actual institution, but when others restrictively manage and organize your daily life, who would not wish for greater independence? As with all the themes from your study, the imagined narrative[3] you created to summarize the participants' experiences with independence provided me with a look into the past, while showing me what is powerfully present today (Gordon, 2008). You captured the essence of human wants in this way:

> We badly want to be more independent than we can be here. We want to be able to stay home alone, go out by ourselves, and we feel good when we can spend money the way we want. It also feels good to own a lot of things, things that other people use. Owning a car or just to be able to drive would make some of us feel very independent. Some of us want a job in the community, but we all want to get out of here, not so much because we don't like it here (although sometimes we don't) but because we just want to be on-our-own. We can't stand having to listen to others all the time, sometimes even to people much younger than we are. We don't like being told what to do. Always being with other people, that gets to be a hassle too. We think we are capable of living on our own, with a little help here or there, but that's all right. Everyone needs help sometimes. We want to live alone or with a roommate or marry and be on our own. (Hesushius, 1981, p. 136)

You see, the past remains present (Gordon, 2008), Lous. Even today, the community-based living arrangements for adults with disabilities retain institutionalized characteristics—governing systems of coordinated activities administered by managers and staff members, inflexible schedules, restrictive organization of one's day, and isolation (Sinecka, 2009). This particular theme from your study may be labeled "independence," but I believe your participants may be talking about something akin to interdependence. To live on your own with a little help here or there, because everyone needs helps sometimes.

3.1 *Independence vs. Interdependence*
Merriam-Webster defines independence as "freedom from outside control or support" ("Independence," n.d.). Synonyms include freedom, autonomy, and

RESPECT FOR THE GHOST, JUSTICE FOR THE LIVING 97

liberty. This is what I see your participants describing. The tricky piece is freedom from support. When I think of my own life and I think about "freedom from support" I don't feel free at all—I become anxious. What would my life be like without the support of others? As I type that question I experience fear and I picture myself curled up in a ball of anxiety. Personally, my life is a very interdependent one. But, this letter isn't about me (although, yes a little of it is). So what does it matter if I play sematic gymnastics with words like independence and interdependence?

Well, over the past 40 years I have seen "independence" used as an antonym to freedom, rather than a synonym. Thirty years ago the word was a necessity. It had power in the time of total institutions (Goffman, 1963). Independence meant something. The disability rights movement secured the right to freedom, independence, and autonomy through political action. Part of the larger disability rights movement, the independent living movement was and remains based on the principle that community living should be a choice for *all* people with disabilities, including those most greatly impacted by their impairment. The first Center for Independent Living was founded by disabled activists in Berkeley in 1972, alongside landmark rights legislation including the Rehabilitation Act of 1973, the Education for All Handicapped Children's Act of 1975 (now the Individuals with Disabilities Education Act), and the Americans with Disabilities Act of 1990. Discrimination against people with disabilities has far from ended. Millions of disabled people are forced to live in poverty, residing nursing homes or group homes, despite the revolution inspired by the independent living movement (ILM). To be sure, the ILM transformed lives for many in the U.S. with newly won access to civil rights, to a place in American society, and to the political landscape.

But, like so many other aspects of the disability rights movement, the concept of "independence" has been co-opted by the deficit-driven industries of special education and adult services (later, I will tell you about the similar fate of "self-determination"). I've seen freedom turned into a task analysis, autonomy into a checklist, and liberty as something requiring pre-requisites or evidence. That special education and adult services have co-opted "independence" in such a way, frightens me. I see your participants in those checklists—they haunt the task analysis. Because "independence" has been turned into something so far removed from freedom and liberty, turned into a skill to be learned and mastered. Has it instead, become a roadblock to autonomy rather an emancipatory force?

Your participants felt good when they could spend their money the way they liked. But did they need to fall on the "natural cue" step of the prompt-fade hierarchy in order to buy a new pair of jeans? Did they have to score in the 90th percentile on a battery of life skills assessments in order to move into an apartment with a roommate of their choosing? It's not that there's anything inherently wrong with task analyses and checklists. The travesty occurs when the results of those analyses are used to limit freedom and stifle independence. I see this occur far too often in today's schools when a student's need for support relegates her to the segregated, special education classroom.

I introduced you to Hope earlier in this letter and I bring her up again now, because her life circumstances remind me so of your participants and provide a strikingly clear example of how far we must continue to go. Throughout the three months I spent interviewing Hope, her narrative, too-often, reflected the denial of independent and interdependent living experienced by your participants 30 years ago. In the spirit of imagination and fictive truths grounded in the real, I believe Hope would share a narrative similar to the one that follows. As with your conclusions, Lous, I am offering you an *imagined narrative* containing many phrases actually said by Hope during our time together. Your participants' haunt this narrative. Their spectrality makes plain a segregated system of practices and beliefs that has not entirely gone away (Gordon, 2008).

> *I enjoy food and cooking immensely. I don't get to do this much at home because all of our meals are planned and someone else writes our grocery lists. Sometimes I read aloud a menu or sometimes I stir juice. School is the place where I actually get to cook—not home. I make many choices in my life like what I wear to school, what I eat for lunch, and the after-school activities I do. I don't get to choose my own breakfast since it's already been written for me on our menu. I also don't get to choose where to sit or what classes I take at school. But I am very happy and proud that I got to decide what my job site for my transition program would be. My day at home is pretty structured: we watch television programs, eat at 5:00 pm, and then I go to bed at 7:00 pm.*
>
> *One thing I am really excited about is my summer job. There is a long waiting list at Alliance[4] where I hope I'll be able to work with computers. I didn't choose to work at Alliance, someone chose for me. But I'm choosing to work with computers. My housemate, John, tells me I won't be doing that, because someone else already works in the office ... All of my housemates work at places like Alliance. I started arguing with John about this the other day and my Service Coordinator said maybe they would find a way for me to work in the office. I overheard her say these places involve "piecemeal" work. I'm not sure what that means, but I hope I can work with the computers instead.*

Do you see how your participants haunt the life laid out for Hope? The coordinated and restricted day of a group home and always being around other people, the desire for a job in the community, and the capacity to live on your own "with a little help" but the ultimate denial of this wish. Hope's experiences, as was true with your participants' experiences, were shaped by her institutionalized life. One of her closest friends was her agency-appointed advocate who is also a paid support staff in her group home. Hope had limited access to friends her own age and limited access to her community due to inaccessible transportation. Her meals were planned for her and even though she expressed a strong interest in cooking, her experience was limited to stirring juice.

3.2 *For Her Own Good*

Hope's school day and time at home were very structured and she was in bed by 7:00 pm. She shared with me that she wanted to attend the local community college for nursing and is interested in working with young children. Yet, Hope would begin her piece-rated job at a sheltered work center very soon, a job that was chosen for her by her residential manager. It was quite distressing to see how a 21-year-old young woman's life has unfolded in such an institutionalized manner. What mattered to her was second to what others felt would be enacted for her own good.

The way in which Hope's life unfolds in such a pre-determined way can be explained, in part, by the institutionalized culture of her residential services (Goffman, 1963; Sinecka, 2009). The remnants of total institutions found in today's human services industry shaped the opportunities Hope had for making choices and directing her life in a free and autonomous way. Indeed, Wehmeyer & Bolding (2001) found when adults with intellectual disabilities moved to community-based living and work environments from more restrictive settings, significant changes in autonomy occurred.

I also question the ease with which Hope had moved from one institutionalized setting to the next (a medium-sized group home, to segregated classrooms, to a sheltered workshop). I have been able to find little research to justify adolescents with disabilities living in group homes. Shapiro and Chandler (2012) provided anecdotal evidence of families in similar situations and indicated that 6,000 children under the age of 21 were currently living in nursing homes across the United States. The authors cited medical costs and Medicaid denials as potential reasons for this exorbitant number. I mentioned to you, Lous, that Hope received free and/or reduced lunch while in school, but she was also assigned legal guardianship three years prior to my study. Her guardian obtained a post-baccalaureate degree, but worked multiple part-time jobs. While I hesitate to generalize, I cannot help but ask myself, "Would Hope reside in a group home (at her young age) if her social location reflected an middle- or upper-class background? How can her situation not raise concerns of social justice?" Economic and cultural capital play a significant role in this corporeal haunting.

Can you also see how the segregation of the past continues to linger today? What is being done? History is beginning to arrive at a new future, because hauntings are about transformation as well. The social violence of total institutions and the co-option of independence is slowly being undone.

4   The Undoing of Sheltered Work

As I wrote to you earlier, Lous, there have finally been strides in successfully dismantling one total institution: sheltered workshops. It becomes less and less likely that young people like Hope, and the participants from your study who desperately wanted careers in the community, will remain warehoused in segregated "jobs." Disability rights activists have been fighting for this end for decades. The beginnings of change were seen in 1999 with the Supreme Court case *Olmstead v. L.C.* Brought forth by two women with psychiatric and intellectual disabilities who remained confined to an institution for years after professionals recommended community-based services for them. The court held that,

> ... public entities must provide community-based services to persons with disabilities when (1) such services are appropriate; (2) the affected persons do not oppose community-based treatment; and (3) community-based services can be reasonably accommodated, taking into account the resources available to the public entity and the needs of others who are receiving disability services from the entity. (United States Department of Justice, Civil Rights Division, n.d., para. 2)

The Olmstead decision of 1999 required states to place "qualified" individuals with mental disabilities in community settings instead of institutions. However, even with the establishment of the Olmstead Act (1999), "our federal and state governments continue to uphold an apartheid system of mass congregation and segregation of adults with intellectual and developmental disabilities in sheltered workshops and day activity centers" (Rogan & Rinne, 2011, p. 248).

Shortly after the Olmstead Act (1999), Taylor (2002) cited both pragmatic and philosophical grounds to relegate sheltered workshops to the history books. Describing low pay, the virtually nonexistent likelihood of securing community employment once placed in a segregated setting, and the need for workshops to retain high producing workers, Taylor called for an end to sheltered work. Ten years later, Diament (2012) highlighted the class-action lawsuit of 2,300 adults with developmental disabilities in Oregon indicating, "they're being relegated to sheltered workshops even though they're capable of working in the community" (para. 1). The U.S. Department of Justice even weighed in on the this particular lawsuit arguing the similarity of sheltered workshops to institutions, and stated that the unjustified placement of people with disabilities in congregate work settings when a person could be employed in the community is a sufficient to file claim under the Americans with Disabilities Act.

Finally in 2014, President Obama signed the Workforce Innovation and Opportunity Act. The law makes it more difficult for sheltered workshops to pay subminimum wages to people with disabilities. Greater emphasis is also placed on transition services, career counseling, and vocational rehabilitation (Diament, 2014). But, the proverbial nail in the coffin may have most recently occurred when the 2016 democratic presidential candidate Hillary Clinton committed to eliminating subminimum wage and closing the 78-year-old loophole that allows employers to pay workers with disabilities less than minimum wage due to perceptions of earning or productivity capacity (Marans, 2016). Someone is finally listening. The ghosts are getting their reckoning.

5 The Not-Quite-Reconciled Notion of Independence

Sheltered work is slowing coming to an end across the United States. People are also, slowly rethinking the meaning of independence. Members of the disability justice movement have been pushing back against the "myth of independence" for some time now:

> With disability justice, we want to move away from the "myth of independence," that everyone can and should be able to do everything on their own. I am not fighting for independence, as much of the disability rights movement rallies behind. I am fighting for an interdependence that embraces need and tells the truth: no one does it on their own and the myth of independence is just that, a myth. (Mingus, 2011, p. x)

Disability justice activist Mia Mingus writes of the importance of continuing to address issues of access, but implores us to move away from independence-driven notions of access (which tends to focus more greatly on individualism) to a more collective, interdependence-driven discussion focused on communal support and the reality that no one, disabled, able-bodied or anywhere in-between, goes it alone. Mingus also notes how interdependence allows for greater opportunities to embrace difference rather than assimilation, and a more complex, interconnected disability community.

Some educational researchers have been pushing back against "independence" as a be-all goal for all people with disabilities as well. Scholars such as Harry, Rueda, and Kalyanpur (1999), Smith and Routel (2010), and Trainor (2005) have brought to light this pervasive, Western cultural ideology found in today's special education and adult service industrial complexes. Principles of self-reliance are imbedded in special education practice (Harry, Rueda, & Kalyanpur, 1999), many teachers do not believe that students with significant disabilities can live self-determined lives (Wehmeyer, 2005), and reciprocity and interdependence tend to be largely ignored educational and adult service spaces (Smith & Routel, 2010). All of this continues to occur even when young adults with disabilities share their desire to live close to families for help and support and their need for friends as important sources of emotional and physical support (Cooney, 2002). Together, disability justice activists and scholars are slowly burying the ghosts of "independence" as the pinnacle of an autonomous life.

6   A Conversation on Romantic Relationships

The discourse regarding sexuality and disability is a nuanced and complicated one that is historically charged and reflective of the tensions between hundreds of years of ableist assumptions colliding with the desires, rights, and freedoms of disabled people. According to Ware and Cowley (2015), "cultural messages about sex and disability reinforce the binary concept of people with disabilities as either asexual[5] innocents who cannot have sex, or at the other extreme, as hypersexualized beings who, unless their sexuality is contained and discouraged, will, as adults, pose a menace to society."

The consequences of these cultural messages have been nothing short of ruinous for disabled people, particularly intellectually disabled individuals. Institutionalization, eugenic sterilization, and special education have all done violence in the name of protection: protecting the asexual innocent from the dangers of sexuality and protecting society from the perils of the hypersexualized disabled. With this history in mind and with Gordon's (2008) ghosts haunting my engagement with your book, I looked for evidence of these cultural messages and their violent consequences. It was this story, Lous, that your participants shared, that stood out.

RESPECT FOR THE GHOST, JUSTICE FOR THE LIVING

We want to get married, and most of us will, soon, or in a few years. Some day we will, because it brings the things we want. It will give us a home, companionship, and care, but especially it will take us out of here and then we can be on our own. It will allow us to be involved in sexual behavior, and that must be very exciting. I do know about sexual behavior that involves more than holding hands or giving a kiss, and I'll engage in it when I'm married (especially intercourse, that would be bad to do now), but it does sound exciting, and, actually, I can't wait till I am married so I can find out more about it ... We do feel somewhat tense and anxious about it, though. It is all rather confusing. We can't do it, yet we get all the messages about how exciting it must be. The television tells us so, the movies, pictures in books, remarks made by staff, words in songs we hear. It must be an important thing in life. But we can't have it; one must be married and we cannot marry here. Thus it is normal for us that we can't engage in it. We must not be ready for it ... If our present boy/girlfriend leaves, we will take another one, for it is important to keep believing that we, too, can marry and live on our own one day, and do the things we want to do, just as everyone else. (Hesushius, 1981, pp. 136–138)

Forty years ago, the participants in your study revealed their want for companionship, sexual intimacy, and marriage. However, the historical materialism of sterilization coupled with institutional and heavily managed, group home living arrangements, wrapped in a discourse of patriarchal protectionism resulted in the socially violent denial of access to sexuality and reproduction. Desire for independence was denied. Desire for sexual intimacy was denied. Desire denied. The opportunity to be involved in a romantic relationship was, and continues to be closely monitored by families, the human services industry, and the state.

For your participants, marriage appeared to be a gateway to more than sexual intimacy alone. Marriage meant freedom, leaving the institutionalized life of the group home, and agency. The hegemony of all of this is not lost on me, Lous. During my initial reading of these narratives, I understood the "sex-only-after-marriage" message to reflect abstinence-only discourses. I understood the oppressive discourse, which would lead a disabled person to frame marriage as the only avenue to experience sexual intimacy. It was at the time and remains to this day, the discursive script that shapes the sexual lives of students, young adults, and "single ladies." Abstinence-only sex education and sex-after-marriage advice continues to have a stronghold in the U.S. But, the "sex-after-marriage" message shared by your participants was much more complicated than this.

The participants in your book and even across the research studies that you cited pointed to the message that "marriage *is* for me, even though I'm disabled." I asked myself whether or not marriage was a truly viable option for people labeled intellectually disabled and living in a group home in 1981. Statistics on marriage rates for people with intellectual disabilities are difficult to find to this day, but research by Cohen (2014) indicates that 30% of White, cognitively disabled people marry, while only 15% of Black cognitively disabled people marry, compared to a 72% marriage rate among all people. Surely if it is rare for people with intellectual disabilities to marry today then it had to be even more so in 1981, right, Lous? *No, Danielle! No.*

7 The Myth of Progress and the Criminalization of Sexuality

Drawing on literature from that era (Edgerton, 1967; Gebhard, 1973; Henshel, 1972; Mattinson, 1970) you cite several instances of people with intellectual disabilities marrying. The marriage rates included 62% of participants in Edgerton's (1967) study, 56% of participants from Farber's (1968) study, and 40% of participants from the study by Henshel (1972). So, why was I so shocked to read this? Why did I find it so hard to believe that we had regressed on this particular front: sexuality, intimacy, marriage, etc.? I can't deny that advances have been made over the past 30 years in the field of disability. Americans were rocked by the abuses uncovered at institutions and the vast majority of them have now closed their doors. Students with disabilities have the right to a Free and Appropriate Public Education, and an inclusive life is becoming a reality for more and more intellectually disabled people. But just because a society makes advances does not mean we have plotted a linear trajectory toward "progress."

Gray (2004) has steadfastly debunked the myth of progress for over a decade. Societal, moral, political improvements may be real, but they are also temporary. According to Gray, "history is not progress or decline, but recurring gain and loss" (p. 155). History is cyclical, rather than linear. The current U.S. financial system, climate change denial, globalization, and the corporatization of education all stem from a belief in progress that may be more of an illusion (Hedges, 2014). Hedges begs us to ask, "what losses come from all of these gains?" I, myself, had taken up the illusion of progress when reading your book. Then I tried to understand why.

Regulations abound in the field of special education and in the adult service industry. Labeling practices exist in order to qualify for Special Education services and supports. The art of teaching is often drowned in a sea of bureaucratic paperwork and immense pressures of IEP compliance. I don't mean compliance with the rights entitled to students with disabilities, but compliance as a checklist and a paper trail. Intelligence testing or medical diagnoses are required in order to qualify for Medicaid-funded supports and services. Adults with disabilities who marry risk losing Social Security Income due to "marriage penalties" or losing Medicaid benefits if incomes and assets exceed eligibility levels. Even in the wake of the landmark case of Obergefell v. Hodges (2015) when the U.S. Supreme Court ruled that the Equal Protection Clause of the 14th Amendment guarantees same-sex couples the fundamental right to marry, people with disabilities found themselves, again, at the margins.

In a recent op-ed for the Advocate, disabled trans lesbian Jordan Gwendolyn Davis (2015) explains how she is unable to marry her also disabled partner, as they would be hit with a 25% reduction in Supplemental Security Income benefits. Even if her partner was not disabled, Davis' own benefits could be reduced or eliminated, as her partner's income would be "deemed" to her, no matter how separate the two kept their financial resources. The issue of marriage equality for people with disabilities is much larger than the SSI "marriage penalty." Evans (2012) shares that disabled couples are denied over 1,100 rights when they are denied the opportunity to marry: "they have been denied access to their loved ones hospital rooms, faced family disputes over wills and have been denied spousal benefits from their partner's workplace or government in the event of their partner's death" (para. 1). You see, Lous, this is why I found it so hard to believe that marriage could be a reality for your participants decades ago, but not today?

Like Gray (2003) says, "reoccurring gain and loss." Deinstitutionalization and the memories of abusive horrors led to much regulation in the adult services world—regulation that was intended to prevent the repeat of history. But would Hedges (2014) call this progress? Would Gordon (2008) call this justice for the ghost? I believe the answer would be "no" when one takes a closer look. Because some regulation serves as more than oversight of service providers, it is the oversight of the bodies and actions of disabled people as well that seems of little consequence to many. Take for instance, New York State Office for Persons with Developmental Disabilities (OWPDD, 2011) regulations for "Incident Reporting" and "Considerations for Consent to Sexual Contact," which at best, regulate the bodies of intellectually disabled people, and at worst, criminalize such bodies.

Policy guidance from OWPDD (2011) indicates that some people with intellectual disabilities clearly understand the nature of a sexual relationship, while some clearly cannot or do not have the ability to understand the nature of a sexual relationship. Guidance further indicates,

> ... there is an even larger segment of the population in facilities for whom a more formal evaluation process is necessary ... The evaluation of a person is a highly individualized process that is based on clinical expertise; upon staff's knowledge of the person and personal observation; and the input of significant others, including family members and guardians ... The final evaluation is a professional process involving professional judgments. (pp. 282–283)

Antiquated policies such as these put people with intellectual disabilities in a position to have to *prove* their capacity for sexual consent. Keep in mind that the State Handbook cited above was most recently revised in 2011, but guidance documents regarding sexual consent found in the appendices were dated 1993.The ableist guidance provided above, where formal evaluations, professional processes, and professional judgments are privileged in the name of agency oversight, not only has the potential to oppress sexual expression (Ware & Cowley, 2015), but criminalizes such behavior as well.

OWPDD (2011) defines sexual abuse as "any sexual contact between persons receiving services and others, or among persons receiving services, is considered to be sexual abuse unless the involved person(s) is a consenting adult ... Sexual contact is defined as the touching or fondling of the sexual or other intimate parts of a person, not married to the actor" (p. 52). The state outlines several pages of guidance for agencies responding to sexual abuse, as well as guidance regarding actions to take when the abuse is forced or coercive. Unwanted sexual content, sexual harassment, sexual assault, and rape are serious offenses requiring serious action for anyone, disabled or not. But the guidance documents and decision-making processes described are riddled with references to whether or not the "initiators" or "non-initiators" are capable of consent. Based on that determination, different actions are warranted ranging from contacting local law enforcement to report a criminal act to reporting a "sensitive situation."

For a time, I was responsible for investigating allegations of sexual abuse. But after reading the three-pages of guidance on reporting sexual abuse and the five-page appendix on capacity to sexual consent, even with a Ph.D. in Special Education I would not always know how to respond and I certainly don't agree with the possible responses provided. Why is there not a decision-making option provided for two individuals who *mutually* initiate sexual contact? Why is "dirty talk" reported as psychological abuse? A person with an intellectual disability who has been deemed by a "professional" without an intellectual disability as not capable of sexual consent, can't even *talk* about sex? If both individuals are determined to be incapable of consenting to sexual activity, which doesn't only include sexual intercourse, but other types of sexual activity as well, I need to file an allegation of sexual abuse and I might need to call the police. While these regulations may have been intended to prevent sexual abuse and to protect someone believed to be vulnerable to coercion, the language and actions also patronize people with intellectual disabilities, criminalize their sexuality, and limit the pursuit of an intimate relationship.

8   The Hegemonic Hold of Marriage

Guidance documents provided by the state (OWPDD, 2011), clearly privilege marriage when granting capacity to people with intellectual disabilities. First, marriage gives you an automatic pass into the realm of sexuality. Even sexual contact as defined by the state does not apply to married couples. I interpret that, Lous, as the state removing themselves from the beds of people with intellectual disabilities, but only once they are married. Second, marriage provides you with the assumption of competence. According to the OWPDD, "for persons who are married, there is the assumption that they have the ability to consent to sexual contact" (p. 285). Even back in 1981, your participants knew this, Lous. The equation was simple: I can get married because I am deemed competent. If I am competent that means I can leave this place, live on my own, and have sex if I want to. It's as if the participants in your study were reciting state regulations!

But the hegemony of marriage wasn't just present in state regulations. In 1981, marriage was one of the few viable ways to live the interdependent life that many of your participants wanted—the collective, supportive reality advocated by today's disability justice activists. As you noted: "Marriage, after all, is a socially accepted way of managing one's life through cooperation and help from another; such help is not identified as lacking competency" (Hesushius, 1981, p. 49). It is no wonder that the participants in your study privileged the institution of marriage so greatly. One participant from my study, Victoria, privileged marriage as well.

I have a long-time boyfriend named Geoff. Someday we want to get married and have a home together too. We talk on the phone every day after school, do the Special Olympics together, and we even travelled to New York City together with our families. My family is supportive of our relationship, but sometimes they tease me about it. I don't really like the teasing, so I just ignore it. We spend time together at each other's houses and we know about sexual behavior too. That's what we do sometimes: our love stuff. We kiss and all that stuff, doing things with our bodies. We can keep doing our love stuff once we get married. And I'll be Mrs. Oak, since we'll be married. That's my boyfriend's last name. It's important for me to get married to Geoff and continue our relationship. I hope our families continue to support this choice of ours in the future.

Victoria is able to have a healthy, supported, heterosexual relationship with her boyfriend Geoff. She wants to have a home too. She wants to get married. She wants sexual behavior, companionship, and care. She has some of this now. Nonetheless, Victoria's dream is not a simple one of love and marriage. The shadowy grip of the State holds tight to this dream. Even though Victoria's caring and intimate relationship with her boyfriend moves disabled sexuality away from the margins, their story remains closely tied to the capacity narrative of yesterday and the regulated, patronizing narrative of today. When I met Victoria the "love stuff" she described did not mean sex, but it probably will someday. Will she undergo the scrutiny of the professional gaze and have her capacity for sexual consent questioned? Will her body be regulated and criminalized by the State? Or will Victoria and Geoff become part of the larger disability justice movement where disabled activists like Mingus (2011), are offering new narratives of communal, interdependence or like Davis (2015) and Evans (2012) who are petitioning to remove the State's "marriage penalties."

9   Making Disabled Sexuality Visible

I asked those questions, Lous, because Gordon (2008) asserts that, "we need to know where we live in order to imagine living elsewhere. We need to imagine living elsewhere before we can live there" (p. 5). Throughout your book, Lous, you shared how your participants "lived" in regard to sexuality. And I've shared with you how the shadows of that history shape where the participants in my study live now. But I also want to share with you how people with disabilities are imagining a new place to "live." How they are wrenching themselves away from the hold of the State and re-imagining transgressive narratives of disabled sexuality. Disabled activists, scholars, and even pop culture icons have

RESPECT FOR THE GHOST, JUSTICE FOR THE LIVING 109

taken it upon themselves in recent years to make visible a new story of disabled sexuality, where sexuality is not only a normal, typical part of life, but a human rights issues as well.

Take, for instance, the participatory action research of Kathleen Sitter (2015). She and 12 participants with intellectual disabilities were able to co-create a video-campaign on various aspects of sexuality rights, including human rights, the role of advocacy, histories, barriers, required supports, relationships, and life stories. Videos were shared with the larger social supports community through presentations, workshops, and virtual screenings. Through a critical disability studies and Freirien framework, participants were able to reclaim a history that is often sidelined in the professional literature, lead discussions in their community about sexuality, and create a space for human agency.

Disabled activist and blogger Cara Liebowtiz has also been reimagining the meaning of sexuality for people with disabilities. In her 2015 post to "Everyday Feminism," Liebowitz shares a story of finding her sexual identity, which she describes as "asexual spectrum" through the burgeoning internet-based spaces where marginalized groups have begun finding community. She also warns of the horizontal oppression that many disabled asexual people are currently faced with—the ways in which disabled sexuality movements tend to ignore asexuality and how asexuality remaining classified as a psychiatric disorder reinforces the stigma of disability and the marginalization of people who actually do identify as *disabled* and asexual.

In order to combat this marginalization, Liebowitz (2015) offers several suggestions. First, that people use "some" statements. Instead of blanket statements such as, "disabled people aren't asexual" or "asexual people aren't disabled," we can change our language: "Most disabled people aren't asexual, but there are some disabled asexual people. Many disabled people want sex, and we can run the gamut of all sexual orientations, including asexuality" (para. 63). We must also do a better job of recognizing intersectionality and the multiple ways in which people can experience marginalization. Making intersectionality a priority can make for a more welcoming community with greater access all around.

10   A Conversation on the Self and Choice

I'd like to talk with you, Lous, about the final theme from your study: interpersonal understandings. You described your participants' stories of self-knowledge, choice, loneliness, and the possibility for a different future.

> We know that we are in a place for "the retarded" and we know there are things we cannot do (such as reading, writing, cooking good things, and

math) but that does not make us retarded ... Some of us, to tell you the truth, cannot quite figure out why we are here. So, we are not retarded: we are normal. But we are not living like most people do. It is confusing to figure all this out. Most of us have a hard time putting in words what being normal means, but we do know that we want to live differently from the way we do now ... Sometimes things get tough or lonely around here and it is very upsetting and depressing when there is no one to turn to and to depend on. Then you really feel how terribly alone you stand in this world. Then we feel how dependent we really are. We need to keep believing that we have some say over our lives, and that one day, we will be able to make our own decisions, just as other people do. (Heshusius, 1981, pp. 138–139)

The ghosts from your study are "haunting reminders of lingering trouble" (Gordon, 2008, p. xix). They sustained a social violence where they did not have a say over their lives and were not allowed to make their own decisions. It is frightening to read their stories because this violence was not only done in the past, but remains in the present. Victoria, a participant from my study, has begun her own haunting, if one considers that hauntings expose the cracks and the rigging of injustice, shared a similar story as that of your ghosts. Her experiences with self-awareness and choice demonstrate how the social violence of self-determination denied, remains an unresolved issue that begs to make itself known.

My mom told me that self-determination means, "doing what you need to do to get the things you need." I believe that people who are self-determined are activists and advocates who fight for what they want and need. This also means helping others, to carry weight. Everyday things like helping my friends if they drop their books. Self-advocacy also reminds me about an anti-bullying public service announcement I filmed in New York City. The PSA was about ending the use of the "R-word." I filmed a scene where girls tried to be mean and bully me. Mean girls were trying to steal away my bag and I had to tell them, "Please stop." Then in the scene they didn't stop and called me a retard. I know it was just acting, but that word does hurt.

Part of the reason why I did this PSA was because I was bullied in real life at my school. A boy pulled me into the bathroom and started to kiss me. He was also mean to me. So, I started to fight and I yelled for help. I stuck up for myself. My mom doesn't think the school did the right thing after this. They didn't have it on tape so they couldn't prove it happened.

Now I have to stick with a teacher at all times. It's because I'm in Special Education. The teacher needs to watch you. I like it because I don't straggle around the halls like the other kids in my school.

Self-determination also means you make choices. I choose to have good manners and to behave. I also make choices at school. I choose to not talk when the teacher is talking and to raise my hand instead. I choose to be respectful, nice, and to behave. But, I also choose to sing and dance and write.

11 The Disabled-Self Policed

In Victoria's life at school disability means surveillance and exclusion, no matter what terminology we use. Special Education means you need to be with adults at all times. In today's overcrowded schools and classrooms, many students would benefit from smaller class sizes and lower student-to-adult ratios. But if you have a disability label like Victoria, it is about much more than a small class size and increased teacher attention. Those smaller classes are segregated settings. The students are excluded from their peers without disabilities. There may only be 8–12 students in the classroom, but all the students have disability labels, all the adults are special education service providers, and often that classroom is at the end of a hallway, or in its own wing, or the basement. In that classroom of eight students, there may be six adults who enact technologies of surveillance, monitoring, and exclusion disguised as appropriate supports and services.

In the case of inclusive education, general educators may feel relief with the extra help from special education support services personnel, but teachers can become less engaged with students with disabilities as a consequence. Once a paraprofessional is put in place, teachers often relinquish their instruction to the support personnel. The adult monitoring also tends to be more qualitatively extreme in the case of students with disabilities. As Victoria's story demonstrated, she not only had smaller, segregated classes with more adults, but she walked through the hallways with an adult and ate lunch at a table of adults. She shared that because she was in Special Education she needed to "stick with an adult at all times."

Victoria's disability label and her association with special education, has marked her as a student who requires policing. Victoria noted how the special education students had to stick with their teachers at all times and, unlike "the other kids" at her school, shouldn't "straggle." Although Victoria takes comfort in walking the busy halls of her school with an adult, what typical high school experiences is she missing through this monitoring? What opportunities for social interaction in the informal spaces of school are diminished? There is a certain amount of dignity of risk that is not afforded to Victoria, which results in overprotection that can actually lead to more violence rather than prevent it.

12   Self-Determination Denied

But "risk" in the realm of Special Education, is not described in terms of dignity. Instead of administrators and educators supporting Victoria to regain her sense of self and independence, she was scrutinized even more. And what of the boy who assaulted her? His autonomy, his self-determination remained in tack. However, to be a woman with an intellectual disability means that you are an inherent risk. It means that your self-determination is always suspect and always up for restriction. *Your* self-determination is defined only in certain ways—defined by *others*—not by you.

The concept of self-determination was initially intended as a radical human right of people with disabilities to "gain an adequate voice and representation in society" (Nirje, 1972, p. 177). However, the current literature, pervasively and unapologetically defines self-determination for people with disabilities as a skill to be developed or as a deficit to be remediated. Teachers are positioned as scientific technicians and users of professional interventions, who are charged with remediating and correcting deficits and faults related to self-determination. The foundation of this framework makes little to no mention of the ways in which oppressive structures and ableist assumptions impact the ability of a person to live the life they choose. More to the point, there is little space in the current literature for politicized, contextual, justice-oriented understandings of self-determination (Cowley & Bacon, 2012). Only a few researchers promote the idea that to define self-determination in and of itself—from the perspective of anyone other than the person herself—is inherently problematic (Petersen, 2009; Smith & Routel, 2010).

Although learning the skills necessary in order to advocate for one's choices in life is clearly important, Smith and Routel (2010) pointedly note the colonial ideologies that ground the notion of teaching self-determination to others. Self-determination is frequently described as something to be acquired through a step-by-step process in which an individual exhibits certain degrees of self-determination or is provided with tools to become more self-determined (Agran et al., 2000; Wehmeyer et al., 2000). When self-determination is conceptualized as a skill to be taught, rather than a right through we one exercises agency (Smith & Routel, 2010), there is often little to no mention of how dominant ideologies, unjust educational practices, and lack of societal support and response to influence whether or not a person can act with volition or be a causal agent (Thoma, Rogan, & Baker, 2001).

Professional conceptualizations of self-determination also rely heavily on cultural ideologies of independence, individualism, and self-reliance (Harry, Rueda, & Kalyanpur, 1999; Smith & Routel, 2010; Trainor, 2005; Ward, 2005). However, individualism is not a primary value for all people, and independence is a bit of a façade. Most people, disabled or not, tend to live interdependent lives. Yet, the Western emphasis on independence that pervades the self-determination literature helps to create a conflated binary whereby self-determined "equals nondisabled" and not-self-determined "equals disabled." This can most readily been seen in research showing that teachers do not always believe it is important for students with intellectual disabilities to exercise self-determination (Wehmeyer, 2005). This violent belief is unacceptable.

The concept of self-determination must be broadened to more accurately reflect the interdependent nature of all our lives. Smith and Routel (2010) recommend human service and education fields reconceptualize self-determination as a concept that is relative to the individual experiences of each person and his or her family, rather than definitions which may exclude certain demonstrations of agency, competency, and advocacy. Self-determination is not something that can be defined for *others*; it must be defined for *oneself*.

Activism—both in and away from school—was one way in which Victoria constructed her own definition of self-determination. She also constructed self-determination as compliance in school as a young woman who is polite, behaves, follows classroom rules, is respectful toward others, and doesn't get into trouble. Hers was a choice to comply, but this was against the narrative constructed through Victoria's IEP. Her present levels of performance are littered with adjectives describing her as sweet, likeable, polite, kind, hard-working, and she is described as a "happy young lady that [sic] is motivated to do well and to please those around her." This culture of compliance is particularly problematic for young women. Victoria's constructions of self-determination as politeness, following rules, and being nice and sweet, in addition to the value placed on compliance and pleasing others reflect antiquated gender stereotypes that, according to Chenoweth (1996), can contribute to violence against women with disabilities.

Maybe you recognized this too, Lous, but I'm terrified by this culture we have created, dependent as we are upon Special Education and it's abject refusal to recognize the importance of the voice, the desires, the demands of disabled youth in their claims for freedom. Special Education remains forever bound in a culture of compliance, overprotection, and segregation: extreme marginalization that contributes to greater vulnerability for disabled children and youth. A culture that violently denies real self-determination, choice, and freedom, it has created students who define choice as good behavior—seemingly in an effort to claim normalcy that will likely never be in their reach.

Historically, self-determination was not something afforded to your participants. Instead of a reckoning for this injustice, the field of Special Education has forcibly disappeared the political nature of self-determination that so many disabled activists fought tirelessly to uphold. It is because of the disappearance of rights-based, justice orientations of self-determination that young women like Victoria find themselves policed in their schools and made to believe that choice means compliance and politeness. The over-and-done-with is not done. We may have come far in the area of disability rights since 1981, but troubles remain. The echoes of violence and the denial of this fundamental right, linger in the everyday lives of disabled youth. The unresolved social violence experienced by your participants—segregation in a group home, the resultant feelings of terrible loneliness, and the right to decide, to determine the course of one's everyday life as well as the future, denied—is making itself known. Your ghosts, "tie present subjects to past histories" (Gordon, 2008, p. viii).

13   How to Close?

The haunting I experienced while reading your book, Lous, is "forcing a confrontation, forking the future and the past" (Gordon, 2008, p. xvii). How will I respond? Gordon provides some instruction on how to address this imaginary reality of residing with the ghost:

> The ghost registers and it incites, and that is why we have to talk to it graciously, why we have to learn how it speaks, why we have to grasp the fullness of its life world, its desires and its standpoint ... Because ultimately haunting is about how to transform a shadow of a life into an undiminished life whose shadows touch softly in the spirit of a peaceful reconciliation. (pp. 207–208)

She implores us to make a hospitable place for the ghost, while remaining partial to the living. That is my final charge in this letter to you, Lous. I've shared with you how the ghost registers today: community-based living arrangements that retain institutionalized characteristics, task analyzing freedom and autonomy, the criminalization of sexuality, the hegemonic hold of marriage, they ways in which disabled students are policed in schools through labeling and segregation, and how self-determination has been enacted in a colonized manner steeped in White, middle-class ideologies of choice, independence, and success. But I've also written to you about the transformations that are occurring and the confrontations disabled people and their allies are forcing: the undoing of sheltered work, interdependent priorities, sexuality and human rights advocacy, the acceptance of spectrums of sexuality, and the visibility of disabled sexuality through popular culture, and the reconsideration of self-determination through student activism and self-definition.

In this closure, I ask, "*How do I force a confrontation for the living?*" My power currently lies with cultivating perspective and skills development with future teachers. In my university teaching, my students and I address issues of sexuality, transition, human rights, self-determination, and inclusion. I could have chosen task analysis to guide their instruction, but instead we discuss Universal Design for learning, differentiated instruction, inclusive pedagogies and the right to claim identity development informed by disability experience. We struggle together with how to best support students in an interdependent way. We trouble taken-for-granted definitions of self-determination and begin to undo the colonization that has occurred within this human right. We talk about sex. We talk about sex in an empowering, informational, right-based, diverse manner. I talk about sex so much Lous, that I've become the resident expert and am asked to guest lecture on the topic each semester. This is my small way to force a confrontation for the living. This is how the ghost always touches the edges of my work. S/he insures I speak to the horrors of yesterday, the echoes that remain today, and the peaceful reconciliation that has begun. This is how the stories of your participants haunt my work today, and how I teach for justice.

Respectfully yours,

Danielle M. Cowley

Notes

1 During Heshusius' (1981) participant observation study with eight young people labeled "retarded" and living in a group home, she stressed to the participants that she was, "there only to be with them, talk with them, and learn from them" (p. 14). This serves as the inspiration for the structural choice of this chapter. It is organized as a fictitious letter, grounded in real truths, written to Heshusius by me. So, I may talk about the commonalities between the participants in her study and the participants from my 2013 dissertation. To uncover the ways in which these stories

from 1981 have reverberated across advances in justice and continued pitfalls for 30 years.

2 All names and places have been changed.

3 Heshusius' (1981) made the narrative choice of summarizing and concluding the major themes of her study as if the participants spoke/wrote them. The reason for her choice was to provide a more cumulative narrative and "to grasp some of the ways in which meaning was given to living ... to state the findings as these persons might if they could deliberately and reflectively step out of their reality" (p. 136). Her conclusions are written as if spoken by the participants, as many of the phases were actually said.

4 Alliance is a pseudonym for sheltered workshop in Hope's community.

5 It is important that we recognize the place of asexuality along the continuum of sexuality and not erase the existence of asexual disabled people. Not all disabled people, just like not all able-bodied people, want sex (Liebowitz, 2015).

References

Agran, M., Blanchard, C., & Wehmeyer, M. L. (2000). Promoting transition goals and self-determination through student-directed learning: The self-determined learning model of instruction. *Education and Training in Mental Retardation and Developmental Disabilities, 35*(4), 351–364.

Beratan, G. D. (2006). Institutionalizing Inequity: Ableism, racism and IDEA 2004. *Disability Studies Quarterly, 26*(2).

Blatt, B. (1977). Issues and values. In B. Blatt, D. Biklen, & R. Bogdan (Eds.), *An alternative textbook in special education.* Denver, CO: Love Publishing.

Charmaz, K. (2005). Grounded theory in the 21st century. In N. K. Denzin & Y. S. Lincoln (Eds.), *The Sage handbook of qualitative research* (3rd ed., pp. 507–535). Thousand Oaks, CA: Sage.

Chenoweth, L. (1996). Violence and women with disabilities. *Violence Against Women, 2*(4), 391–411.

Clough, P. T. (1994). *Feminist thought.* Cambridge, MA: Blackwell Publishers.

Cooney, B. F. (2002). Exploring perspectives on transition of youth with disabilities: Voices of young adults, parents, and professionals. *Mental Retardation, 40*(6), 425–435.

Cohen, P. (2014, November 24). Marriage rates among people with disabilities (save the data edition) [Web log post]. Retrieved from https://thesocietypages.org/families/2014/11/24/marriage-rates-among-people-with-disabilities-save-the-data-edition/

Cowley, D. M. (2013). *"Being grown": How adolescent girls with disabilities narrate self-determination and transitions* (Unpublished doctoral dissertation). Syracuse University, Syracuse, NY.

Cowley, D. M., & Bacon, J. K. (2013). Self-determination in schools: Reconstructing the concept through a disability studies framework. *PowerPlay: A Journal of Educational Justice, 5*(1), 463–489.

Creswell, J. W., & Pano Clark, V. L. (2011). *Designing and conducting mixed methods research* (2nd ed.). Los Angeles, CA: Sage.

Danforth, S., & Gabel, S. L. (2006). Introduction. In S. Danforth & S. L. Gabel (Eds.), *Vital questions facing disability studies in education* (Vol. 2, pp. 1–16). New York, NY: Peter Lang.

Davis, J. G. (2015, June 29). Op-ed: Why no matter what, I still can't marry my girlfriend. *Advocate.* Retrieved from http://www.advocate.com/commentary/2015/06/29/op-ed-why-no-matter-what-i-still-cant-marry-my-girlfriend

DeVault, M. L. (1999). *Liberating method: Feminism and social research.* Philadelphia, PA: Temple University Press.

Diament, M. (2012, May 1). Feds: Sheltered workshops may violate disabilities act. *Disability Scoop.* Retrieved from http://disabilityscoop.com

Edgerton, R. B. (1967). *The cloak of competence: Stigma in the lives of mentally retarded.* Berkeley, CA: University of California Press.

Evans, D. (2015, June 28). Disabled people penalized for getting married. *Audacity Magazine.* Retrieved from http://www.audacitymagazine.com/disabled-people-penalized-for-getting-married/

Gallagher, D. J., Heshusius, L., Iano, R. P., & Skrtic, T. M. (2003). *Challenging orthodoxy in special education: Dissenting voices.* Denver, CO: Love Publishing Company.

Gebhard, P. H. (1973). Sexual behavior of the mentally retarded. In F. F. de la Cruz & G. D. La Veck (Eds.), *Human sexuality and the mentally retarded.* New York, NY: Brunner/Mazel.

Giangreco, M. F. (2003). Working with paraprofessionals. *Educational Leadership, 61*(2), 50–53.

Go, M. L., & Otvertchenko, D. (Producers) & Tate, J. (Director). (2015). *Guest room* [Motion picture]. US: Cicatrice Pictures.

Goffman, E. (1963). *Stigma: Notes on the management of spoiled identity.* New York, NY: Simon & Schuster.

Gordon, A. F. (2008). *Ghostly matters: Haunting and the sociological imagination.* Minneapolis, MN: University of Minnesota Press.

Gray, J. (2004). Heresies: *Against progress and other illusions.* London: Granta.

Harry, B., Rueda, R., & Kalyanpur, M. (1999). Cultural reciprocity in sociocultural perspective: Adapting the normalization principle for family collaboration. *Exceptional Children, 66*(1), 123–136.

Hedges, C. (2014, January 26). The myth of human progress and the collapse of complex societies. *Truth Dig.* Retrieved from http://www.truthdig.com/report/page3/chris_hedges_jan_27_column_transcript_collapse_of_complex_societies_2014012

Henshel, A. M. (1972). *The forgotten ones: A sociological study of Anglo and Chicano retardates.* Austin, TX: University of Texas Press.

Heshusius, L. (1981). *Meaning in life as experienced by persons labeled retarded in a group home: A participant observation study.* Springfield, IL: Bannerstone House.

Hesse-Biber, S. N. (2007). Feminist research: Exploring the interconnections of epistemology, methodology, and method. In S. N. Hesse-Biber (Ed.), *Handbook of feminist research: Theory and praxis* (pp. 1–26). Thousand Oaks, CA: Sage.

Independence [Def. 1]. (n.d.). *Merriam-Webster online.* Retrieved from http://www.merriam-webster.com/dictionary/independence

Individuals with Disabilities Education Improvement Act of 2004. (2006). Pub. L. No. 109–476.

Liebowitz, C. (2015, November 12). 3 ways you might be marginalizing disabled asexual people (and what to do about it). *Everyday Feminism.* Retrieved from http://everydayfeminism.com/2015/11/marginalizing-disabled-asexuals/

Marans, D. (2016, March 29). Hillary Clinton takes a stand against 'subminimum wage' for people with disabilities. *Huffington Post.* Retrieved from http://www.huffingtonpost.com/entry/hillary-clinton-subminimum-wage-people-with-disabilities_us_56faf630e4b083f5c605ef20

Mattinson, J. (1970). *Marriage and mental handicap.* Pittsburgh, PA: University of Pittsburgh Press.

Mertens, D. M. (2005). *Research and evaluation in education and psychology: Integrating diversity with quantitative, qualitative, and mixed methods* (2nd ed.). Thousand Oaks, CA: Sage Publications.

Mingus, M. (2011, February 12). Changing the framework: Disability justice: How our communities can move beyond access to wholeness [Web log post]. Retrieved from https://leavingevidence.wordpress.com/2011/02/12/changing-the-framework-disability-justice/

New York State Office for Persons with Developmental Disabilities (OWPDD). (2011a). *Incident management community of practice: Meeting minutes.* Retrieved from http://www.opwdd.ny.gov/sites/default/files/documents/incident_management_minutes.pdf

New York State Office for Persons with Developmental Disabilities (OWPDD). (2011b). *Part 624 handbook: Reportable incidents, serious reportable incidents, and abuse.* Retrieved from http://www.opwdd.ny.gov/sites/default/files/documents/maual_part624_handbook.pdf

Nichols, M. (2016, March 9). What "guest room" really says about disability [Web log post]. Retrieved from http://www.meriahnichols.com/guest-room/

Nirje, B. (1972). The right to self-determination. In W. Wolfensberger (Ed.), *Normalization: The principle of normalization in human services* (pp. 176–193). National Institute on Mental Retardation.

Obergefell v. Hodges (Director), Ohio Department of Health et al. (2015, April 28–June 26). Certiorari to the United States Court of Appeals for the Sixth Circuit No. 14–556. Argued April 28, 2015 – Decided June 26, 2015[1].

Olmstead v. L. C. (98–536) 527 U.S. 581. (1999). Retrieved from http://www.law.cornell.edu/supct/ html/98-536.ZS.html

Peterson, A. J. (2009). Shana's story: The struggles, quandaries and pitfalls surrounding self- determination. *Disability Studies Quarterly, 29*(2).

Rogan, P., & Rinne, S. (2011). National call for organizational change from sheltered to integrated employment. *Intellectual and Developmental Disabilities, 49*(4), 248–260.

Shapiro, J., & Chandler, K. (2012, October 16). Disabled kids living isolated lives in institutions. *National Public Radio.* Retrieved from http://www.npr.org

Sinecka, J. (2009). *Agency within constraints: How the agency of people labeled with developmental disabilities is constructed in supported living schemes* (Unpublished doctoral dissertation). Syracuse University, Syracuse, NY.

Sitter, K. C. (2015). Disability, sexual health, and participatory video: Advocating for sexual rights. *Cultural and Pedagogical Inquiry, 7*(1), 1–15.

Smith, D. E. (2005). *Institutional ethnography: A sociology for people.* Lanham, MD: AltaMira Press.

Smith, P., & Routel, C. (2010). Transition failure: The cultural bias of self-determination and the journey to adulthood for people with disabilities. *Disability Studies Quarterly, 30*(1).

Taylor, S. J. (2002). Disabled workers deserve real choices, real jobs. *The Center for an Accessible Society.* Retrieved from http://www.accessiblesociety.org

Thoma, C. A., Rogan, P., & Baker, S. R. (2001). Student involvement in transition planning: Unheard voices. *Education and Training in Mental Retardation and Developmental Disabilities, 36*(1), 16–29.

Trainor, A. A. (2005). Self-determination perceptions and behaviors of diverse students with LD during the transition planning process. *Journal of Learning Disabilities, 38*(3), 233–249.

United States Department of Justice, Civil Rights Division. (2011). *Statement of the department of justice on enforcement of the integration mandate of Title II of the Americans with Disbailities Act and Olmstead v. L.C.* Retrieved from https://www.ada.gov/olmstead/q&a_olmstead.htm

Ward, M. J. (2005). An historical perspective of self-determination in special education: Accomplishments and challenges. *Research & Practice for Persons with Severe Disabilities, 30*(3), 108–112.

Ware, L., & Cowley, D. (2015). Disability and silences that do not tell. In J. Hall (Ed.), *Female students and cultures of violence in the city*. New York, NY: Routledge.

Wehmeyer, M. L. (2005). Self-determination and individuals with severe disabilities: Re-examining meanings and misinterpretations. *Research & Practice for Persons with Severe Disabilities, 30*(3), 111–120.

Wehmeyer, M. L., & Bolding, N. (2001). Enhanced self-determination of adults with intellectual disability as an outcome of moving to community-based work or living environments. *Journal of Intellectual Disability Research, 45*(5), 371–383.

Wehmeyer, M. L., Palmer, S. B., Agran, M., Mithaug, D. E., & Martin, J. E. (2000). Promoting causal agency: The self-determined model of instruction. *Exceptional Children, 66*(4), 439–453.

Wendell, S. (1996). *The rejected body: Feminist philosophical reflections on disability.* New York, NY: Routledge.

Wendell, S. (2006). Toward a feminist theory of disability. In L. J. Davis (Ed.), *The disability studies reader* (2nd ed., pp. 243–256). New York, NY: Routledge.

Index

ableism   21, 90, 92, 95
access   ix, 4, 17, 19, 22, 31, 32, 82, 92, 93, 97, 99, 101, 103, 105, 109
agency   2, 65, 93, 99, 103, 106, 109, 112, 113
Allan, J.   6
Applied Behavior Analysis (ABA)   5, 32, 41, 43
"aporia"   58, 67
Attention Deficit Hyperactivity Disorder (ADHD), 64, 66,
autism   5, 32, 41, 60
autistic person   60

Baglieri, S.   38, 50
Ballard, K.   3, 40, 41, 44, 45, 49, 54
behaviourism   11, 12
Bernstein, B.   59
Beyond Drill and Practice   17
"Big Glossies"   59
Blatt, B.   19
boundary work   62
Brantlinger, E.   vii, 19, 38

Cara Liebowitz   109
Center for Independent Living   97
choice   21, 51, 52, 59, 76, 83, 91, 95, 97–99, 108–116
community   viii, 1, 2, 5, 13, 20, 28–31, 93, 96, 97, 99, 100, 101, 102, 109, 114, 116
complexity   14, 42
consciousness   6, 7, 27, 35, 36, 38, 62, 63, 73, 77, 79, 81–85
counter narrative   11, 23, 49
Cowley, D.   7, 102, 115
critical special education   vii, ix, 4, 18, 24, 76
curriculum   4, 13–15, 17, 21, 23, 31, 50

deconstruction   6, 37, 44, 45
deficit model   ix, 58
Derrida, J.   58, 67
deskilling teachers   15, 23
"difference as problem"   7
disability studies   3, 4, 6, 8, 22, 26, 66, 109
Disability Studies in Education   vii–x, 4, 6, 7, 18, 22–24, 34, 76, 90,

disability-rights attorney   28
disablement   50, 52, 65, 66
discourse   6, 30, 43, 56, 59, 102, 103
discrete trials   32, 41, 42
dogmatic   57

Edgerton, R.   2, 19, 104
Education for All Handicapped Children's Act of 1975/Individuals with Disabilities Education Act), and the Americans with Disabilities Act of 1990   97

embodiment/embodied   5, 30, 38, 45, 47, 49
epistemological   28, 29, 40, 44, 45, 53, 57, 91
epistemological incongruence   5, 40, 41, 44, 47, 48,
epistemology   73, 76
eugenics movement   94
Exceptional Children   20, 22, 23
exclusion   33, 47–49, 52, 68, 69, 84, 91, 111

family   5, 11, 28, 41, 43, 50, 105, 106, 108, 113
Ferguson, D.   85
Ferguson, P.   85
Finkelstein, V.   65
Foucault, M.   69
fragmentation   17, 52
functional skills   31, 32

Gage, N. L.   19,
Gallagher, D.   6–8, 30
Gordon, A. F.   94, 99, 102, 105, 108, 114
Griffin, S.   53
group home   1, 2, 19. 81, 83, 90–92, 94, 95, 97, 99, 100, 103, 104, 114, 115
Guba, E. G.   18, 19

Hacking, I.   60
Harry, B.   102
Heshusius, L.   vii, 1–8, 10, 13–16, 19–23, 26–30, 32, 33, 35–38, 40, 41, 44–47, 49, 51, 53, 54, 56–58, 60–63, 67, 68, 73–85, 115, 116
holism   4, 10–13, 23, 54

INDEX

housemates 94, 98
humanity 4
humanness 5, 28–33, 95

Iano, R. 23
ideological 4, 5, 13, 33, 57, 91
inclusive education ix, 29, 34, 38, 72, 73, 76, 84, 85, 111
independence 93, 94, 96–98, 100–103, 112, 113, 115
Individual Education Plan (IEP) 4, 16, 17, 27–29, 31, 50, 105, 113
inequality 57, 68
institutionalization 94, 96, 102
intellectual disability 28, 31, 32, 94, 107, 112
interdependence 96, 97, 101, 102, 108
interpretivism 6, 40, 41, 44, 54
interpretivist(s), 19, 75, 76
intersectionality 92, 109
invisible lives 91

justice ix, 66, 67, 89, 91–93, 100–102, 105, 107, 108, 112, 114–116
justice pedagogy 16

Kalyanpur, M. 102

learning 4, 10–17, 19, 21, 23, 29, 31, 32, 42–44, 46, 51, 52, 56, 57, 64, 66, 84, 85, 91, 93, 95, 112, 115
Learning Disability Quarterly (LDQ) 11, 12, 20, 22
Lincoln, Y. S. 18
listening (listen, *really* listen) 2, 4, 6, 19, 36, 46, 47, 57, 58, 60–63, 66–68, 101
LOGO 16, 17

method 1, 2, 6, 11, 18, 19, 32–34, 36, 38, 42, 43, 72–77, 79, 82–85, 92
Mills, C. W. 58, 65, 67, 68
mind-body connection 46, 79
Mingus, M. 101, 102, 108
multiparadigmatic shift 13

narrative vii, 3, 11, 23, 28, 47, 49, 60, 94–96, 98, 103, 108, 113, 116
neoliberal policies 58
Newtonian mechanistic paradigm 28, 31

Oliver, M. 65, 66
Olmstead Act 100

ontological assertions 49, 53
ontological dissonance 49
ontological violence/ontological attack 5, 45, 51
optimism 6, 44, 45, 54
othering 64

paradigm viii, 3, 6, 10, 12–14, 18, 19, 22, 24, 26–38, 40, 44, 45, 76
"paradigm-as-metaphor" 26, 27, 29, 30, 33, 34, 36, 37
paradigm debates 76
paradigm wars 19
paradigmatic assumptions 14, 44
paradigmatic shifts 13, 45
participant observation 19, 81, 90, 115
participatory consciousness 6, 27, 35, 36, 62, 63, 75, 81–83, 85
personhood 91
Poplin, M. S. 11, 13, 14, 23
positivism 3, 6, 12, 15, 17, 19, 40, 41, 44, 54
prescriptive boxed-curriculum 16
professional disillusionment 20

racial inequity 92
reconstruction 6, 44, 45
reductionism 12, 13, 17, 74, 75
reflexive/reflexivity 6, 7, 35, 37, 57, 58, 60, 68
relationships 33, 35, 38, 57, 79, 80, 93, 95, 102, 103, 105–109
research method 1, 2, 18, 19, 75, 76
research participants 2
Rueda, R. 102

school psychologist 5, 30, 51
segregation 34, 38, 91, 92, 100, 114, 115
sel-determination 110–115
"self-in-action" 35, 37, 38
selfother 27, 33, 36, 80, 81
services provision/service delivery 94
Shakespeare, T. 66
sheltered workshops/sheltered work 32, 91–94, 99–101, 115, 116
skills in isolation (isolated skills) 21
Skrtic, T. M. vii, viii, 13, 18, 24
Slee, R. 59
Sleeter, C. 58
Smith, J. K. 18, 75
solidarity 54
special education policy 3
special education practice 20, 22, 102

INDEX 123

special education/teacher education   vii–ix,
       1–4, 6–8, 10–14, 17, 18, 20, 22–24,
       27, 28, 30, 31, 34, 36, 37, 58, 60, 78,
       89, 90, 93–95, 97, 98, 102, 104, 106,
       111–114
Spivak, G.   68, 69
standardization   14, 28, 51
sterilization   94, 102, 103
strategies of (in)difference   64
subjectivity   6, 7, 36, 73, 76–79, 81, 82, 84

task analysis   14, 21, 41, 97, 115
Taylor, C.   80
teachers as technicians   14, 112

teaching   ix, 1, 3, 4, 7, 8, 10–17, 19, 21, 23, 27,
       34–36, 38, 43, 44, 46, 51, 59, 63, 64, 72,
       73, 79, 84, 85, 93, 105, 112, 115
"the inevitable struggle with the self"   27
"the other"   27, 36, 57, 68, 69
the self   27, 31, 33, 35–38, 57, 58, 60, 68, 69,
       79, 80, 82, 83, 93, 109, 113

Vanier, J.   33
violence   5, 45, 48, 49, 51, 53, 91, 93–95, 100,
       102, 110, 112–114

Ware, L.   3–5, 7, 102
Wendell, S.   91